39.95

9/90
STRAND PRICE
$ 22.50

T5-AOK-379

▶The President's backyard, with the Potomac River flowing eastward behind it. In French architect Pierre Charles L'Enfant's original plan for the Mall—the two-mile stretch of grass between the Lincoln Memorial and the Capitol building—the Washington Monument was to have been built on a direct line between the White House and the Jefferson Memorial. Marshy lands doomed the symmetry.

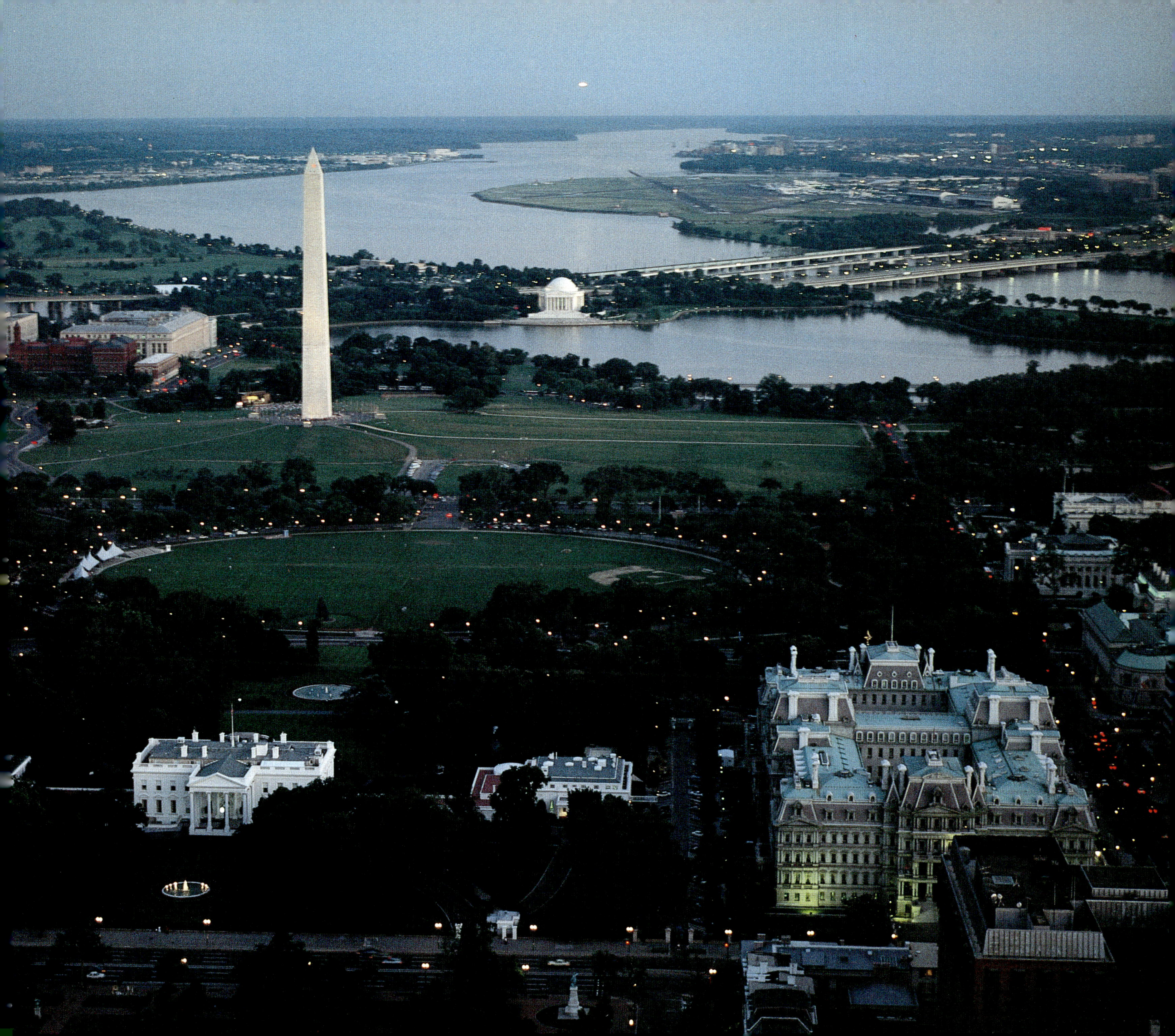

▶ Andrews Air Force Base, Maryland. Opened in 1942 as the Camp Springs Army Air Field, the installation was renamed Andrews Air Force Base in 1947 in honor of Lieutenant General Frank Maxwell Andrews, commander of the United States forces in Europe before his death in 1943. All foreign kings, presidents, premiers, and royalty take their first step on American soil at Andrews. Here, a Senate delegation headed by Louisiana's J. Bennett Johnston returns home from the Soviet Union.

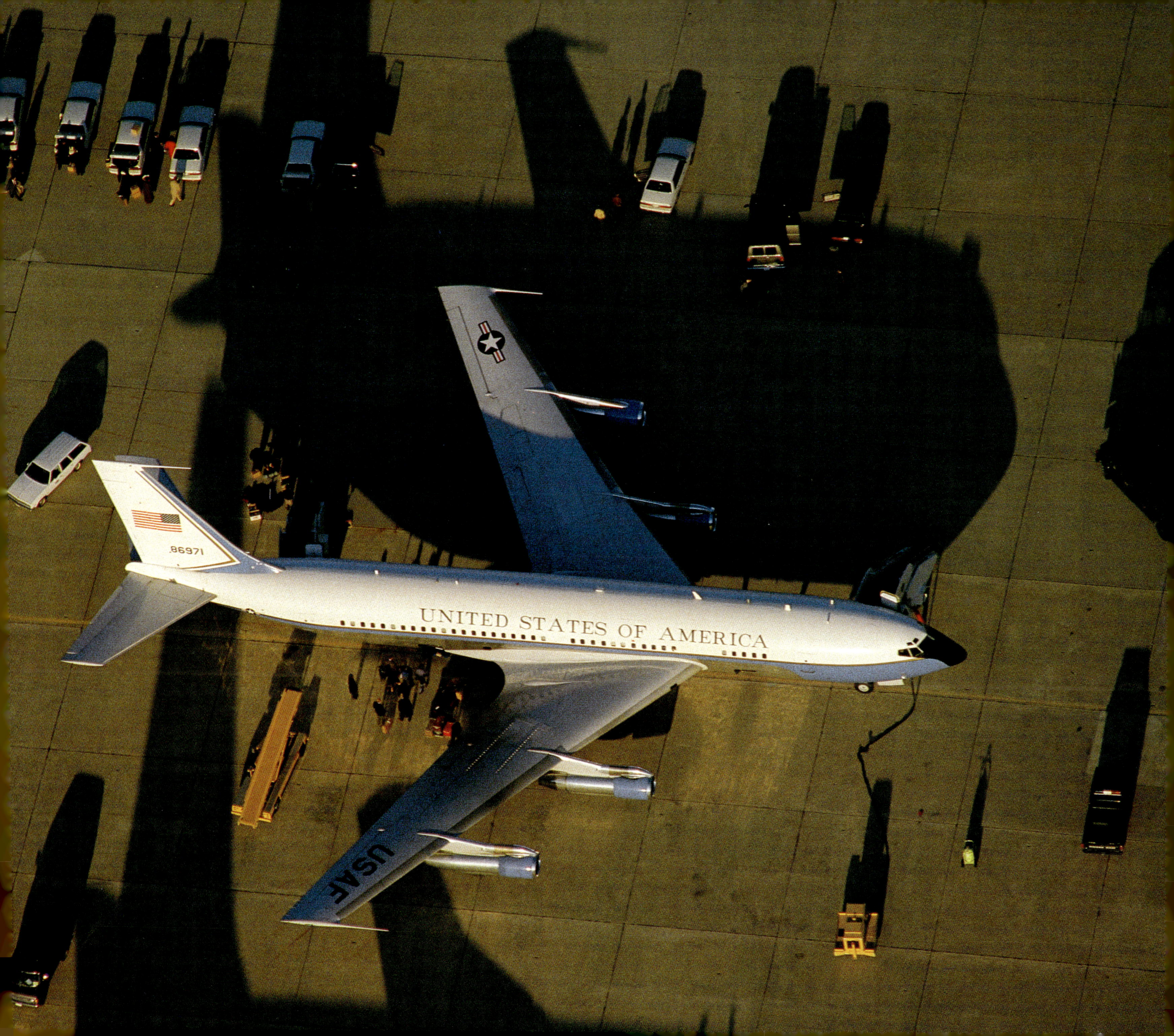
86971
UNITED STATES OF AMERICA
USAF

▶ Picnickers awaiting the 1987 Fourth of July celebration on the Mall. In 1987, 500,000 people descended on the Mall for Fourth of July festivities, which included a large fireworks display. Park police removed the safety glass from the observation windows of the Washington Monument so this photograph could be taken.

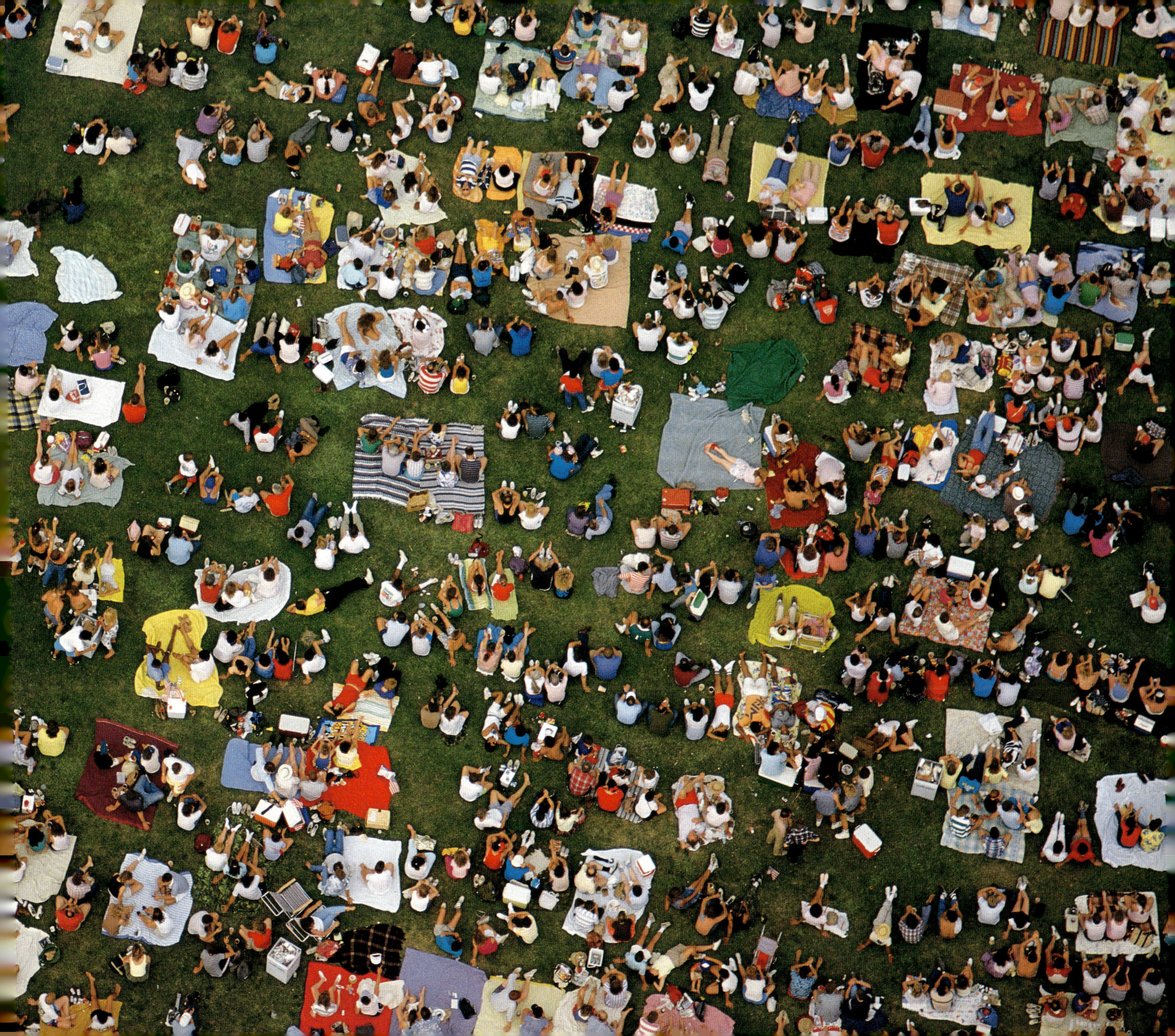

▶Washington at night. Theodore Roosevelt Bridge, seen in the foreground, is one of many bridges heading into the district. Downriver, the lights of two others, the Memorial and Fourteenth Street Bridges, sparkle as a plane takes off from National Airport, while, to the right, the George Washington Memorial Parkway forms a curving ribbon of light.

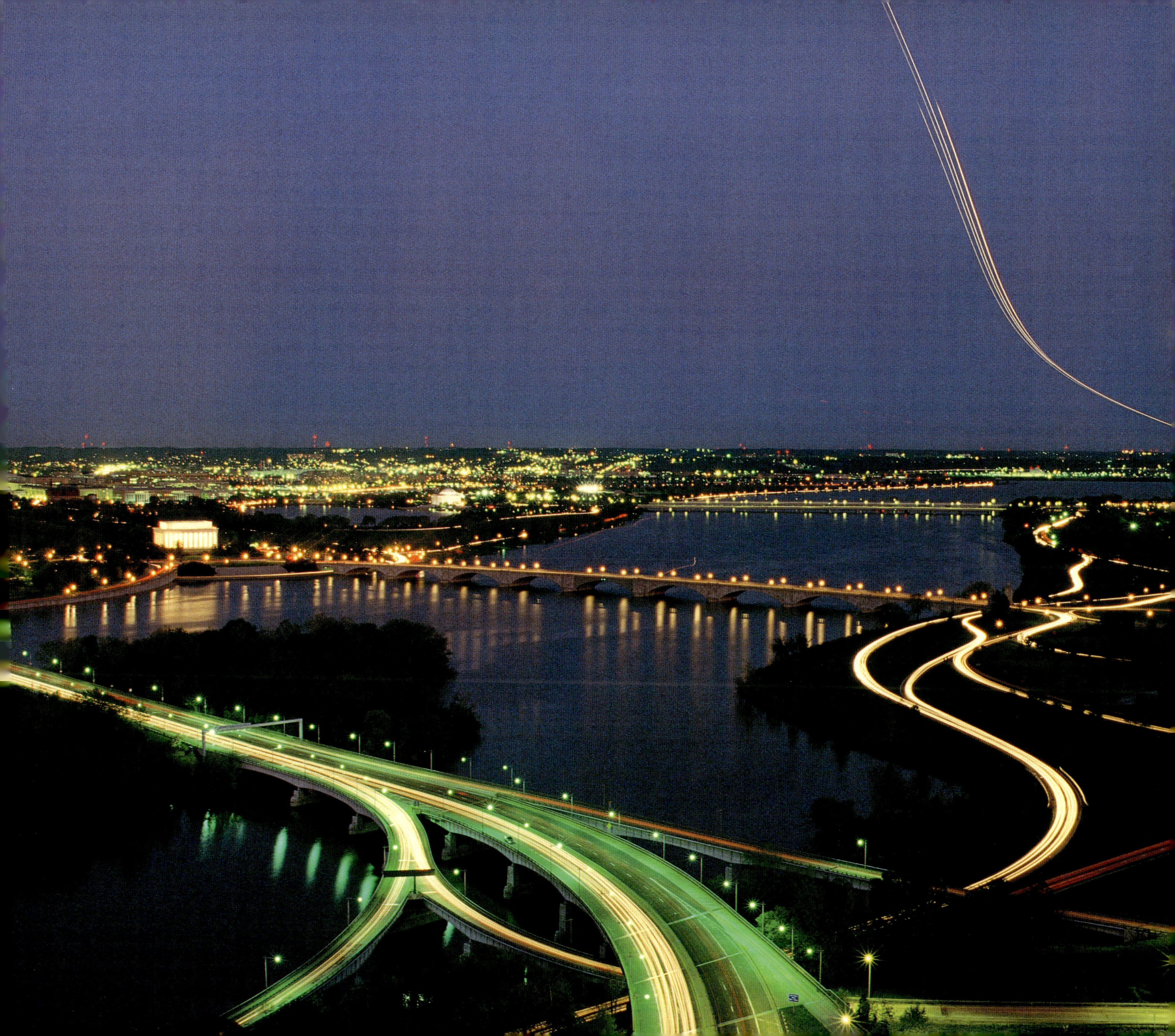

▼ Stone fountain by Daniel Chester French, Dupont Circle. The fountain, a gift of the du Pont family, replaced in 1921 a statue of Rear Admiral Samuel du Pont, a controversial Civil War naval commander, which had stood on the site since 1884. Prior to that time, the location had been known as Pacific Circle.

Designed by Marilyn F. Appleby,
with the assistance of Natalie Hamilton and Josef Beery.
Edited by Kathleen D. Valenzi and Catherine Swift,
with the assistance of Jane Brown and Heather Norton.
Aerial photographs copyright © 1989 by Robert Llewellyn.
Text copyright © 1989 by Howard Means.
All rights reserved.
This book, or any portions thereof, may not be reproduced
or transmitted in any form or by any means,
electronic or mechanical, including photocopying, recording,
or by any information storage and retrieval system,
without permission in writing from the publisher.
Photographs may not be reproduced without permission of Robert Llewellyn.
Text may not be reproduced without permission of Howard Means.
Library of Congress Catalog Card Number 88-80091
ISBN 0-943231-10-8
Printed and bound in Japan by Dai Nippon Printing Co., Ltd.
Published by Howell Press, Inc., 700 Harris Street, Suite B,
Charlottesville, Virginia 22901. Telephone (804) 977-4006.
First Edition

HOWELL PRESS

WASHINGTON

THE DISTRICT AND BEYOND

AERIAL PHOTOGRAPHY BY ROBERT LLEWELLYN

TEXT BY HOWARD MEANS

▶ Lincoln Memorial. Abraham Lincoln had been dead only two years when Congress created the Lincoln Monument Association. Forty-four years later, the monument still incomplete, Congress asked former President William Howard Taft to head a new commission. The cornerstone was finally laid on February 12, 1915; dedication ceremonies were held on Memorial Day 1922. Built at a cost of $2.9 million, the memorial was modeled after the Parthenon in Athens, Greece. It was positioned so that Daniel Chester French's statue of Lincoln can look toward the Capitol.

P laces give up their secrets from the air...and nowhere more dramatically than from above our nation's capital. Seen from on foot or out a car window, a building facade, a row of parked cars, or a tangle of streets at a busy intersection lies hidden as part of a larger scheme. Up high, the camouflage disappears. The plan lays bare. True shape unfolds. What was once a simple facade grows five sides and becomes the Pentagon. Single cars stretch into an automotive distribution center's 45-acre parking lot. A busy intersection becomes a symmetrical panorama of right angles and circles—in Washington, D.C., the possibilities for such transformations are endless.

Unlike the great European capitals from which its first diplomatic residents arrived, Washington, the Brasilia of the eighteenth century, did not accrete over the millenia. It was meant from the beginning to express the raw ambitions of a new nation.

From the air, its blueprint becomes apparent. The gridwork of streets, the radial avenues, the interrupting parks and circles and squares reveal the vision of the federal city's planner, French architect Pierre Charles L'Enfant, as well as that of its founding fathers, George Washington and Thomas Jefferson.

Since its birth, Washington has been a dynamic city, its structure constantly reinterpreted by new planners, new commissions. No city in America, perhaps none in the world, has been so relentlessly plotted. Yet remarkably, with so much change, the fundamental scheme of Washington has endured. By common consent as much as by law, the city has kept a low architectural profile, permitting no building constructed after 1910 to exceed 130 feet. The coherence remains, as Robert Llewellyn's aerial photographs prove. From the exacting symmetry of the Mall, to the more subtle ordering of Beatrix Farrand's gardens at Dumbarton Oaks, Washington blends two worlds—the official, federal city and the unofficial, private one—onto a single realm. By foot, these worlds stun the senses; seen from the air, they stun the intellect too.

Of course, aerial photography is not without its own illusions. As it broadens our perceptions of the ordinary, the everyday, it too becomes a kind of lie, or at least an unreal transformation. Llewellyn's images are no exception.

Truth told, the gate house on the banks of the McMillan Reservoir that appears on page 68 looks quite plain from ground level, the way pedestrians see it. From above, though, bathed in morning light, it becomes almost ecclesiastical—a friary maybe, or some mystical temple along the water's edge. This visual phenomenon occurs time and again on these pages. Buildings, parks, streetscapes—all get lifted out of their ground level contexts, thrown into new ones, rearranged.

Air travelers to Washington know the sensation. Their airplane banks southeast, descending over the Potomac River toward National Airport; for a moment the Washington Cathedral, Georgetown University, the Lincoln Memorial, or some other permanent landmark catches their eye in splendid isolation and grandeur. Then, almost before they know what they have seen, the plane touches down, and the surface world becomes the only world. Here, in this book, Llewellyn's photographs stop the airplane where it was. His photography makes those fleeting moments permanent, indelible.

As natives will tell you, and as the Census Bureau and sometimes grim traffic flow confirm, Washington no longer stops at Interstate 495, the eight-lane highway known as "the Beltway." Appropriately, this photographic portrait of the area moves beyond the Beltway to the sprawling suburbs and farmlands that encircle the capital city. The subject here is the Washington region—from the marinas of Annapolis, Maryland, to the east; the horse-training facilities of Middleburg, Virginia, to the west; and the shopping malls and office parks, cluster housing and the ribbons of asphalt that connect it all. The truth is that the "region" and Washington are one and the same.

Most of the development outside Washington is recent. As late as 1964, the term "Beltway" didn't exist; there was no Interstate 495 to live "beyond." The District of Columbia trailed off into suburban fringe, with the fringe itself giving way to rural farmland. Today, such easy distinctions can no longer be made. Beyond Washington proper lies not a separate community, just a newer one broken here and there by the old country estate — reminders both of what Washington was once and the speed with which, in the ongoing growth of the region, the past is being remade into the future.

Washington remains anchored by its federal center, a national Mall patterned in the shape of a cross. Politicians and residents "inside the Beltway" continue to talk wistfully about a place "outside the Beltway" where, presumably, people with simpler views of the world live, but the distinction strains geography. More and more, where Washington ends in any one direction is anyone's guess. What Llewellyn does so beautifully on the following pages is show you the extent of the possibilities.

◀ U.S. Marine Corps War Memorial in Arlington, Virginia. Felix W. de Weldon's sculpture of Marines planting the American flag on Iwo Jima's Mount Suribachi was based on the Pulitzer Prize-winning news photograph by Joe Rosenthal. Nearly 4,500 American soldiers were killed at Iwo Jima before the Pacific island was declared secure on March 14, 1945.

15

THE DISTRICT

▶ Ionic columns of the Jefferson Memorial. Constructed in the form of a Pantheon to complement the Lincoln Memorial's Parthenon style, the memorial is far more elaborate than Thomas Jefferson would have wanted. Before his death, Jefferson had requested a monument shaped as "a plain die or cube of 3 f., without any moldings, surmounted by an obelisk of 6 f. height, each of a single stone." This request was honored only at Monticello, his Charlottesville, Virginia, estate.

17

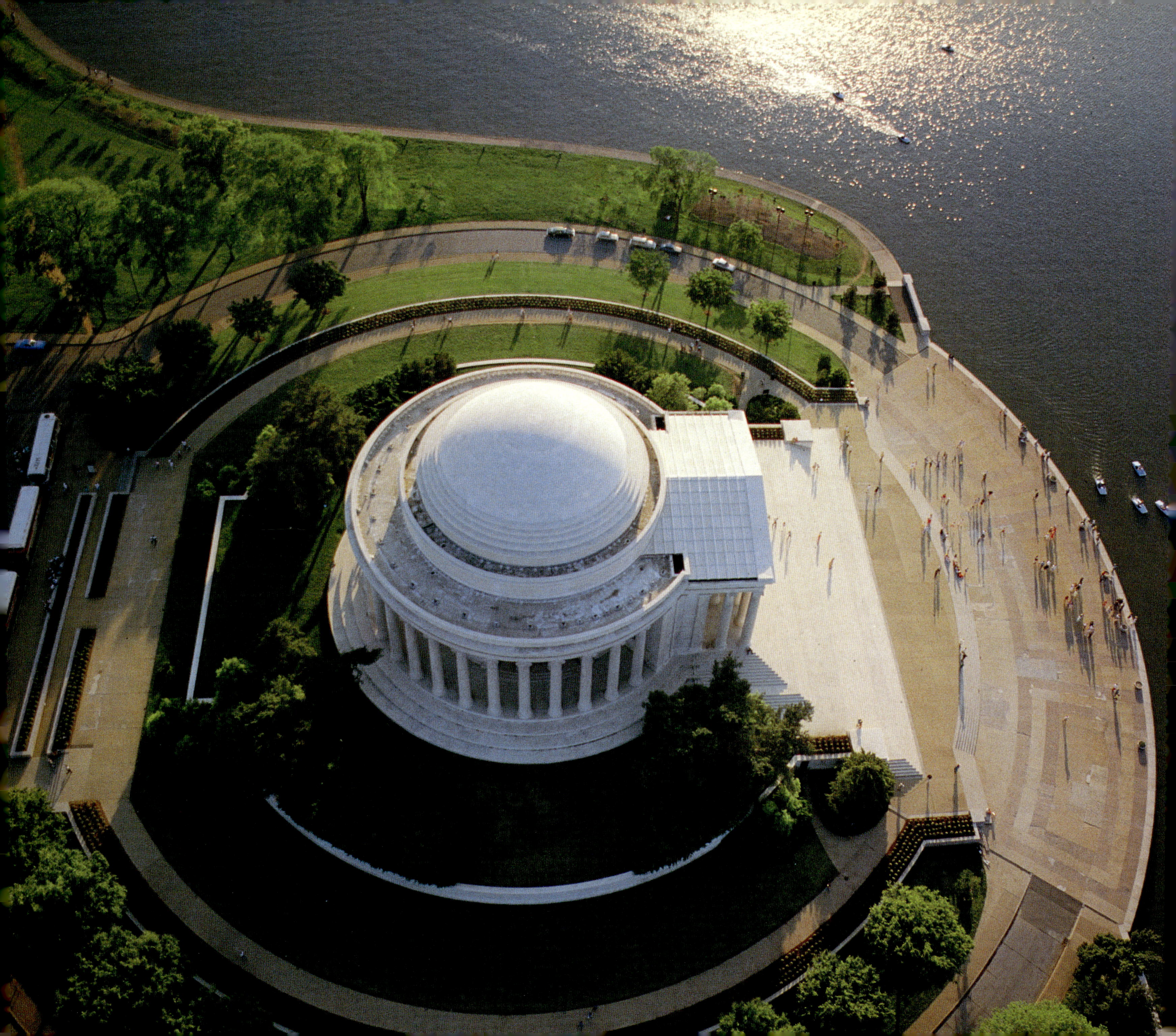

◀▼Jefferson Memorial and paddle boats. The 1902 McMillan plan for the Federal City proposed a generic "Hall of the Founding Fathers." In time the hall came to house only one—Thomas Jefferson. Designed by John Russell Pope, the Jefferson Memorial was dedicated on April 13, 1943, the 200th anniversary of the third United States President's birth. Paddle boats in the Tidal Basin came shortly afterwards.

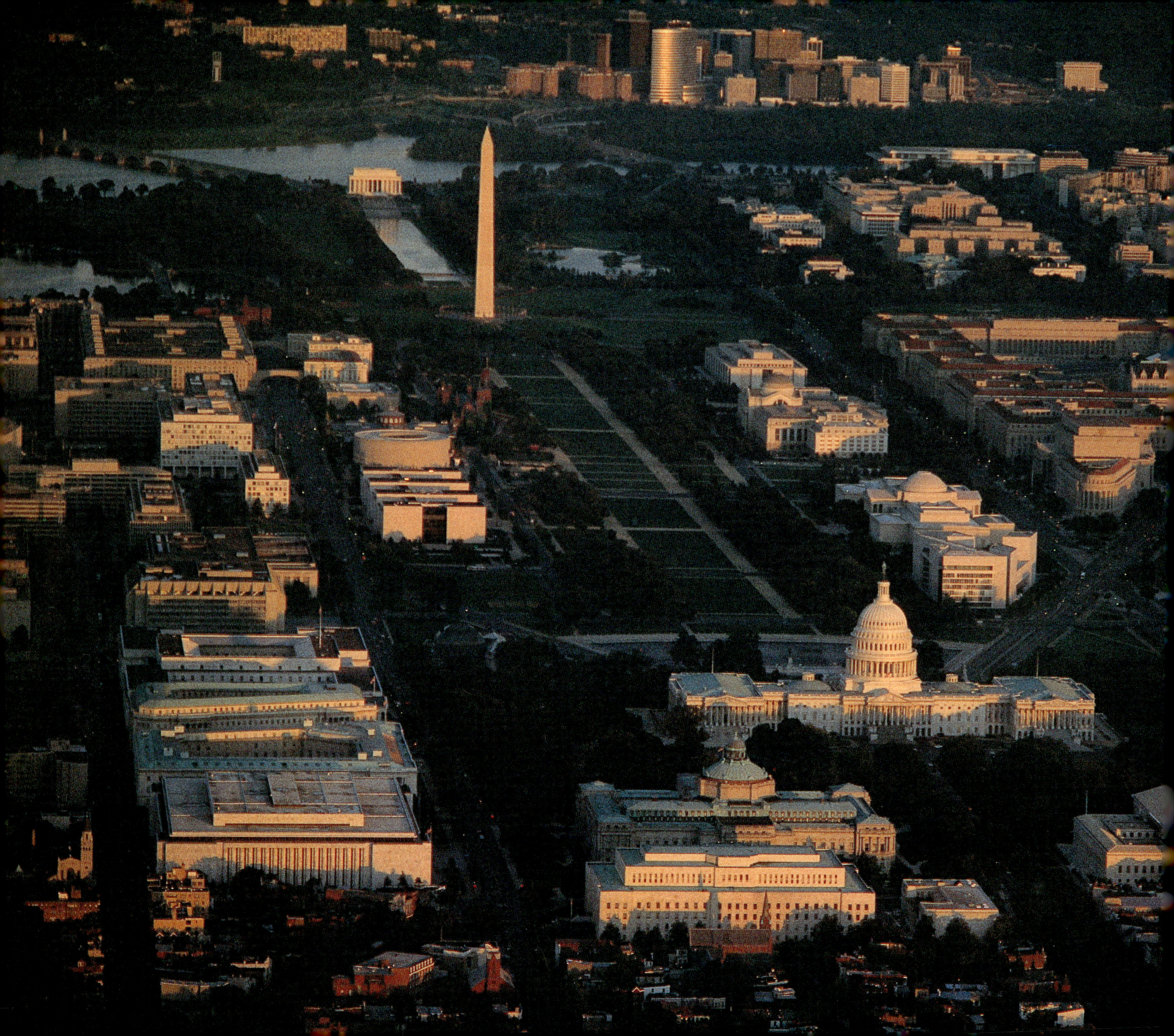

◀ East-to-west view of the Mall. When designing Washington's Mall, Pierre Charles L'Enfant envisioned a "Grand Avenue" 400 feet wide and bordered with gardens and diplomatic residences beyond. William Thornton, the first architect of the Capitol, later proposed that market and fair days be held on the Mall. The Library of Congress, the world's largest repository of books, can be seen in the center foreground.

▲ Dupont Circle Metro station, Q Street entrance. At this subway stop, the escalator that lowers commuters beneath the street is 188 feet 10 inches long—22 feet shy of the Bethesda, Maryland, Metro escalator, which is the world's longest.

▶ Dupont Circle. If the circle were a clock, with noon being top center, Massachusetts Avenue would run from four o'clock to ten o'clock through the circle's center. A commercial hub today, Dupont Circle was once the *sine qua non* of Washington residential life. This part of Massachusetts Avenue—nicknamed "Embassy Row"—was for many years the center of local diplomatic life. The quest for more space, however, has pushed several of the major embassies out to more distant points.

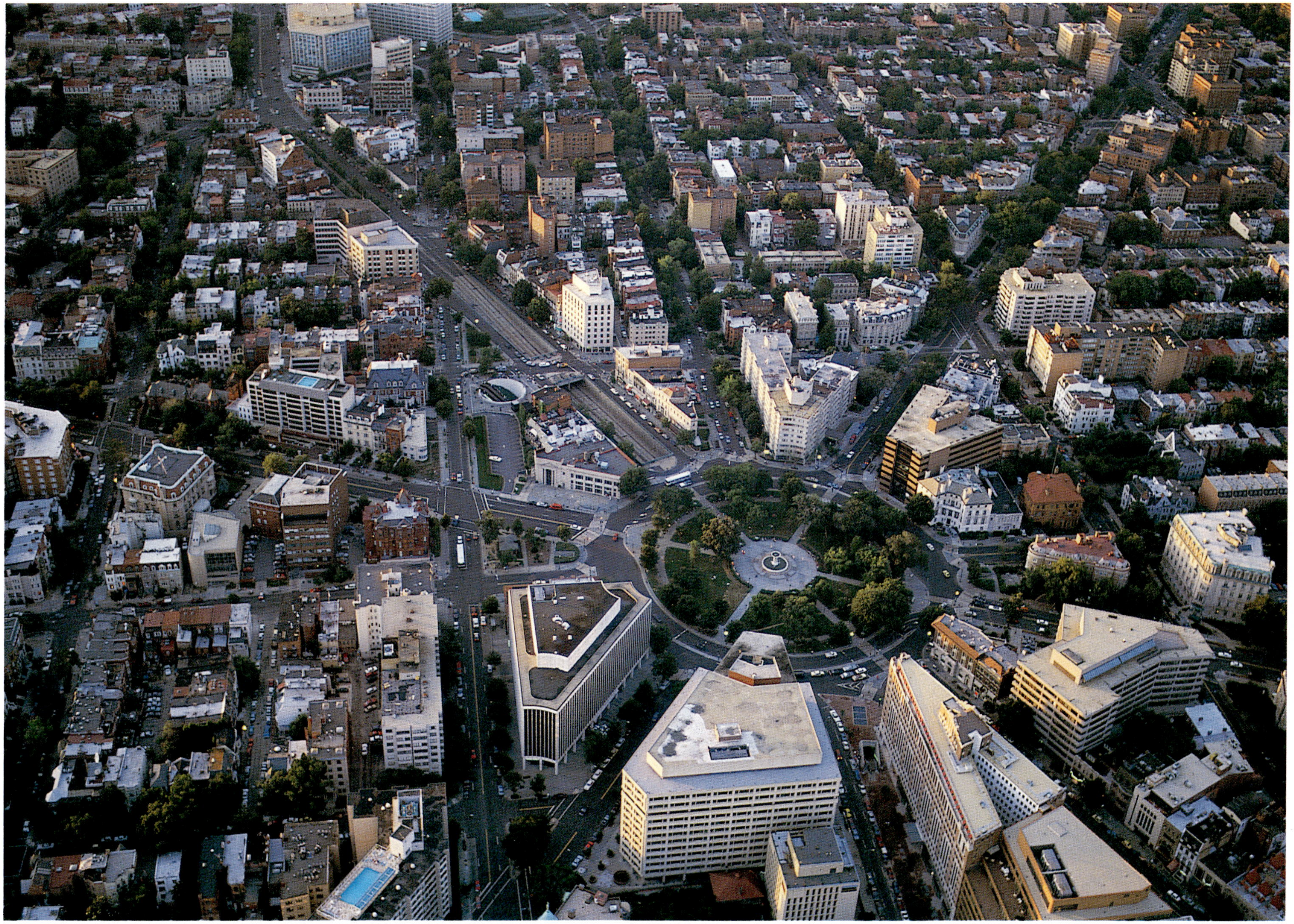

▲ Museum of Natural History, the Smithsonian Institution. Beneath the museum's central dome lies a 71-foot-wide Rotunda, home to a stuffed African elephant. Shot in Angola in 1955, the beast is the largest elephant specimen known to man. Its tusks weigh 96 pounds each; its skull, nearly a ton.

▲ East Building, the National Gallery of Art. Completed in 1978, the East Building is constructed of pink marble from the same Tennessee quarry that provided the stone for the Gallery's West Building. Beneath the crossbar of architect I.M. Pei's "H" sits Henry Moore's 15-ton "Knife Edge Mirror Two Piece," so named because it was designed in two pieces and mirrors, at larger scale, a similar piece created for a London park.

▲ Rainbow Pool. Fourth of July fireworks are being readied for launching in the 1987 version of the annual shoot-off. That year the display lasted 35 minutes, cost the federal government $95,000, and included 12,000 pounds of explosives and more than 4,500 shells, some as heavy as 25 pounds.

▶ Washington Monument and the Reflecting Pool. Seen twice — once in the nearly 2,000-foot-long pool and again standing in solo neo-Egyptian splendor — the monument to the first President was a long time coming. In 1783 the Continental Congress requested that an equestrian statue of General Washington be erected. Sixty-five years later, the cornerstone was laid. Another 37 years passed before the monument — equestrian no more — was dedicated. Built on a 13½-foot-thick slab of concrete, the obelisk rises more than 555 feet into the air. Its walls, 15 feet thick at the base, taper to 18 inches thick at the top.

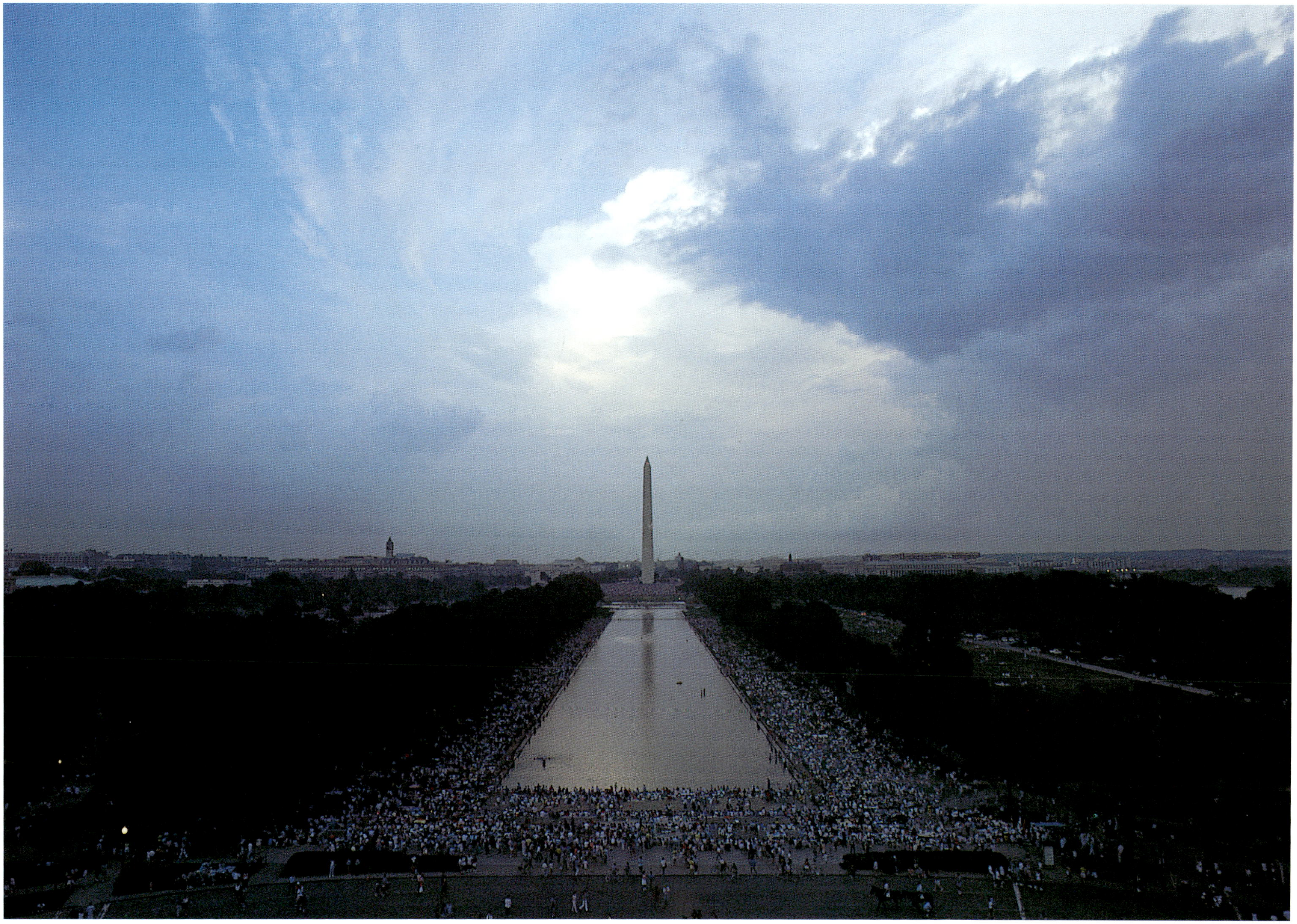

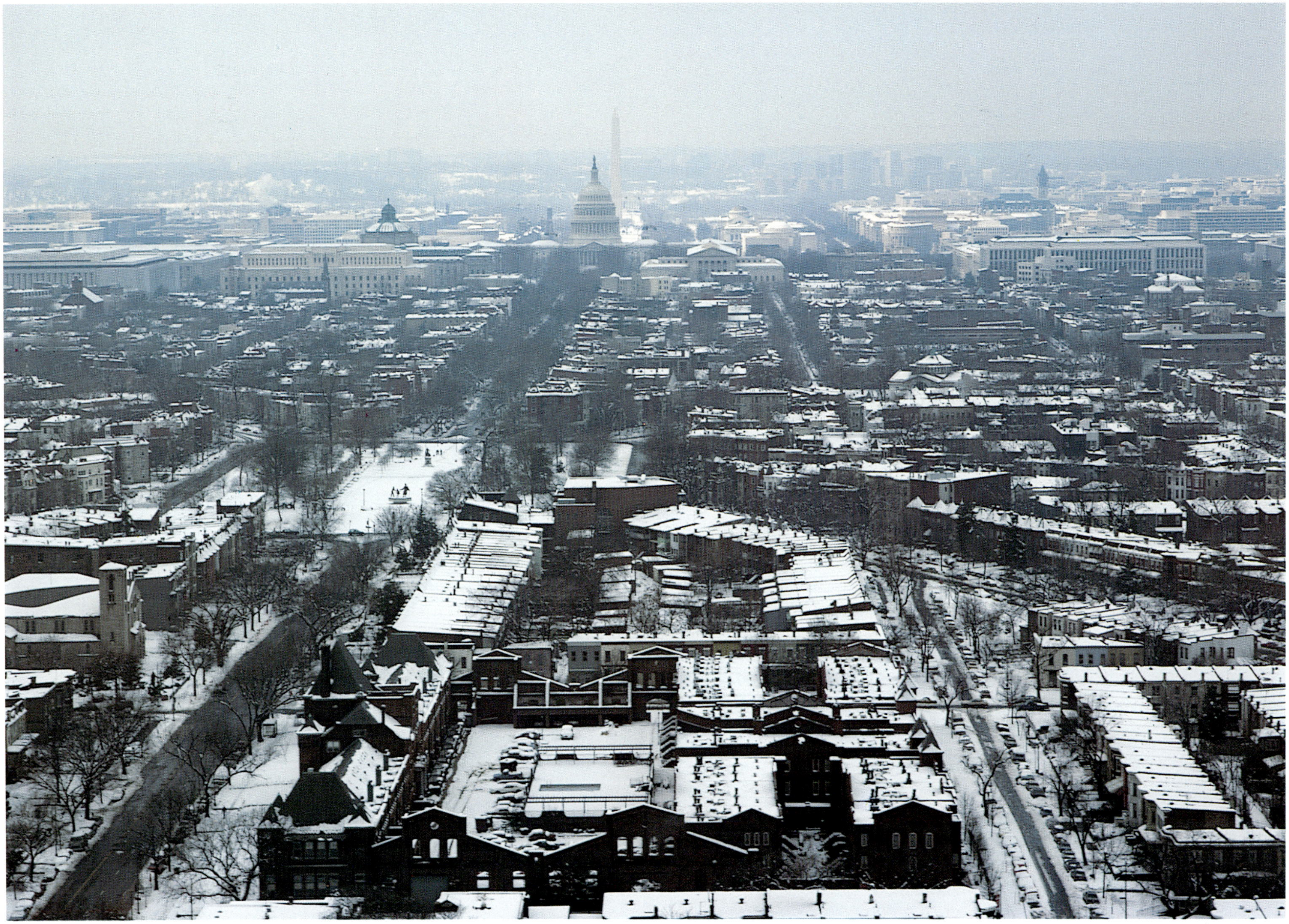

◀Congress's backyard. East Capitol Street stretches from the lower left up toward the Capitol building and is only a shadow of the wide avenue conceived by Pierre Charles L'Enfant, who had envisioned a street paved on each side and shaded by "an Arched way, under whose cover, Shops will be most conveniently and agreeably situated." In Lincoln Park, which interrupts the flow of East Capitol Street, "an historic Column" from which "all distances through the continent are to be calculated" was to rise. Frantic real-estate speculation put an end to the eastern part of the French planner's vision.

▶Arlington National Cemetery, Virginia. Once the estate of Robert E. and Mary Custis Lee, the grounds were converted to a military burial ground during the Civil War in order to inter the men who had died at the hands of Lee's forces. More than 200,000 graves dot the 570-acre cemetery. Some hold the remains of former slaves from the Freedmen's Village that once stood nearby. At the present rate of 15 burials a day, the cemetery's remaining 40 acres will be filled by the year 2020. When that day comes, additional land is expected to be requisitioned from neighboring Fort Myer.

▲▶ Arlington Memorial Bridge and the Jefferson Memorial portico steps. First proposed by Daniel Webster, Memorial Bridge was completed in 1932. Its low lines — designed by the architectural firm McKim, Mead, and White — had two purposes. The first was to protect the view of the Lincoln Memorial, as well as the entrance to Arlington National Cemetery, which is located at the bridge's south end. The other was to avoid interfering with the flight plans of the new air machines then beginning to be a common sight above the Potomac River.

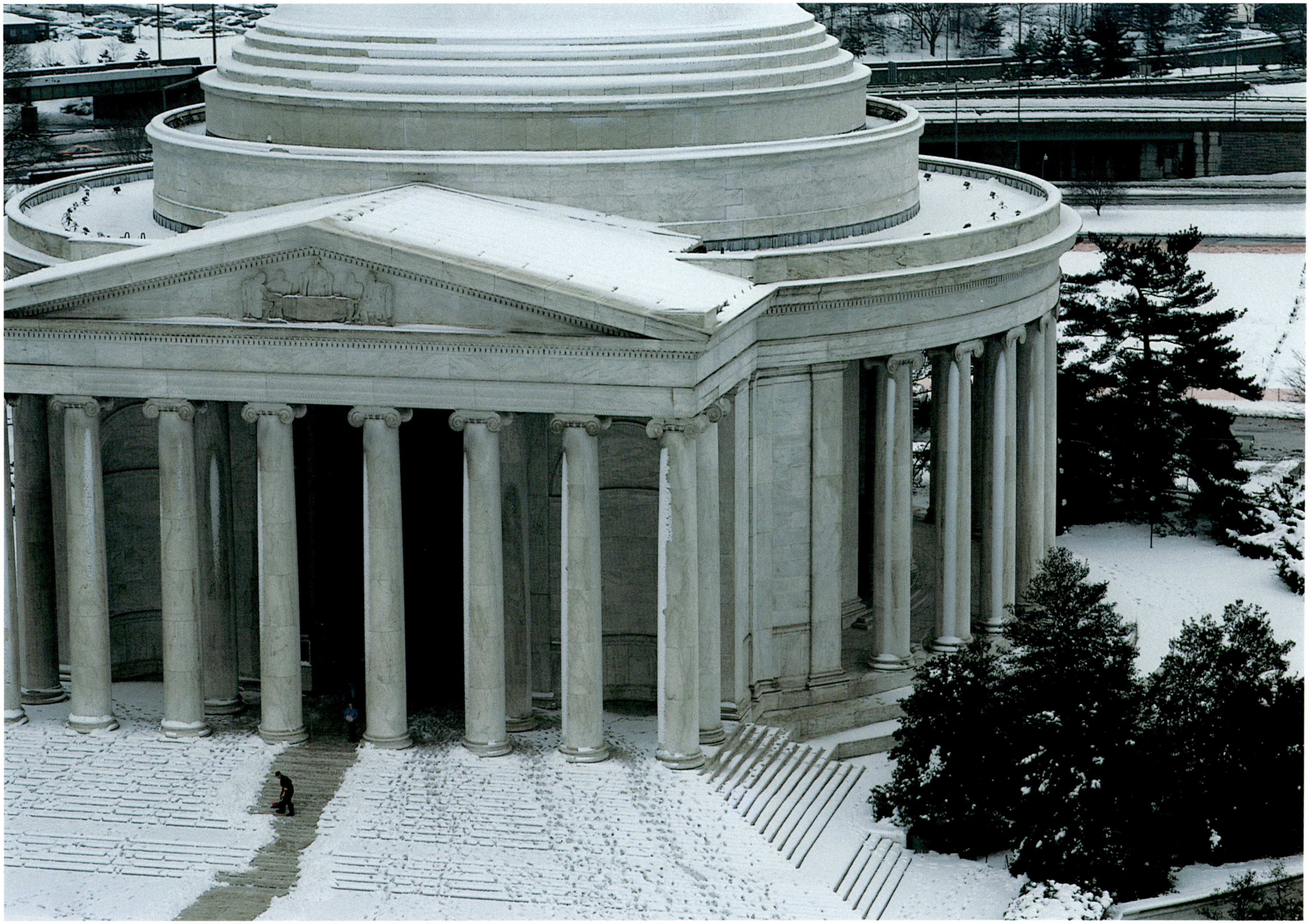

▶ The Capitol. Situated on more than 120 acres, the Capitol is surrounded by grounds planned largely by Frederick Law Olmstead. George Washington laid the cornerstone for the domed structure on Jenkins Hill, as the area was then known, in 1793. Two decades later, a British expeditionary force headed by General Robert Ross reduced the Capitol to ashes. Standing atop the dome is Thomas Crawford's 19-foot-high bronze statue, "Freedom," frequently mistaken for an American Indian.

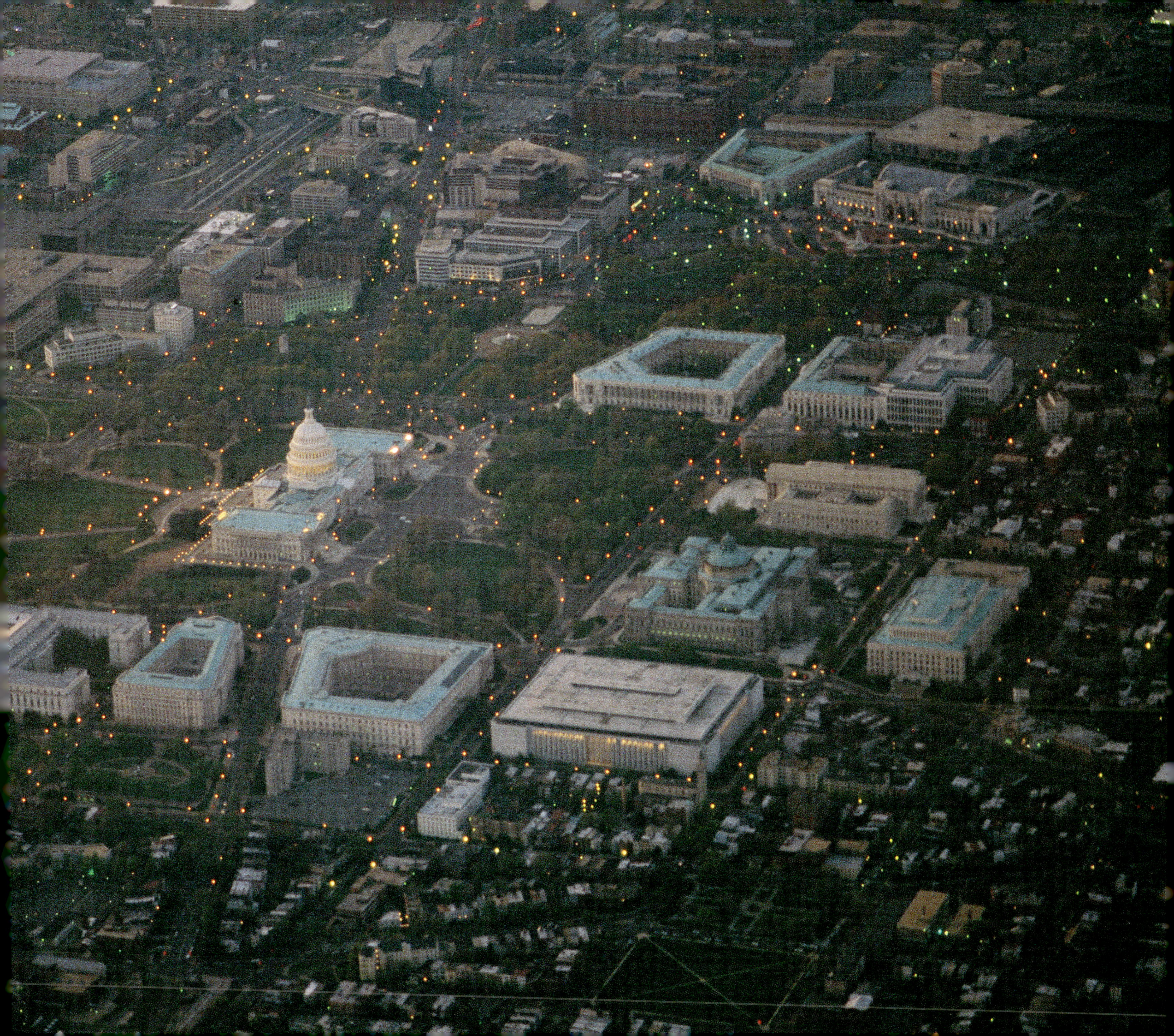

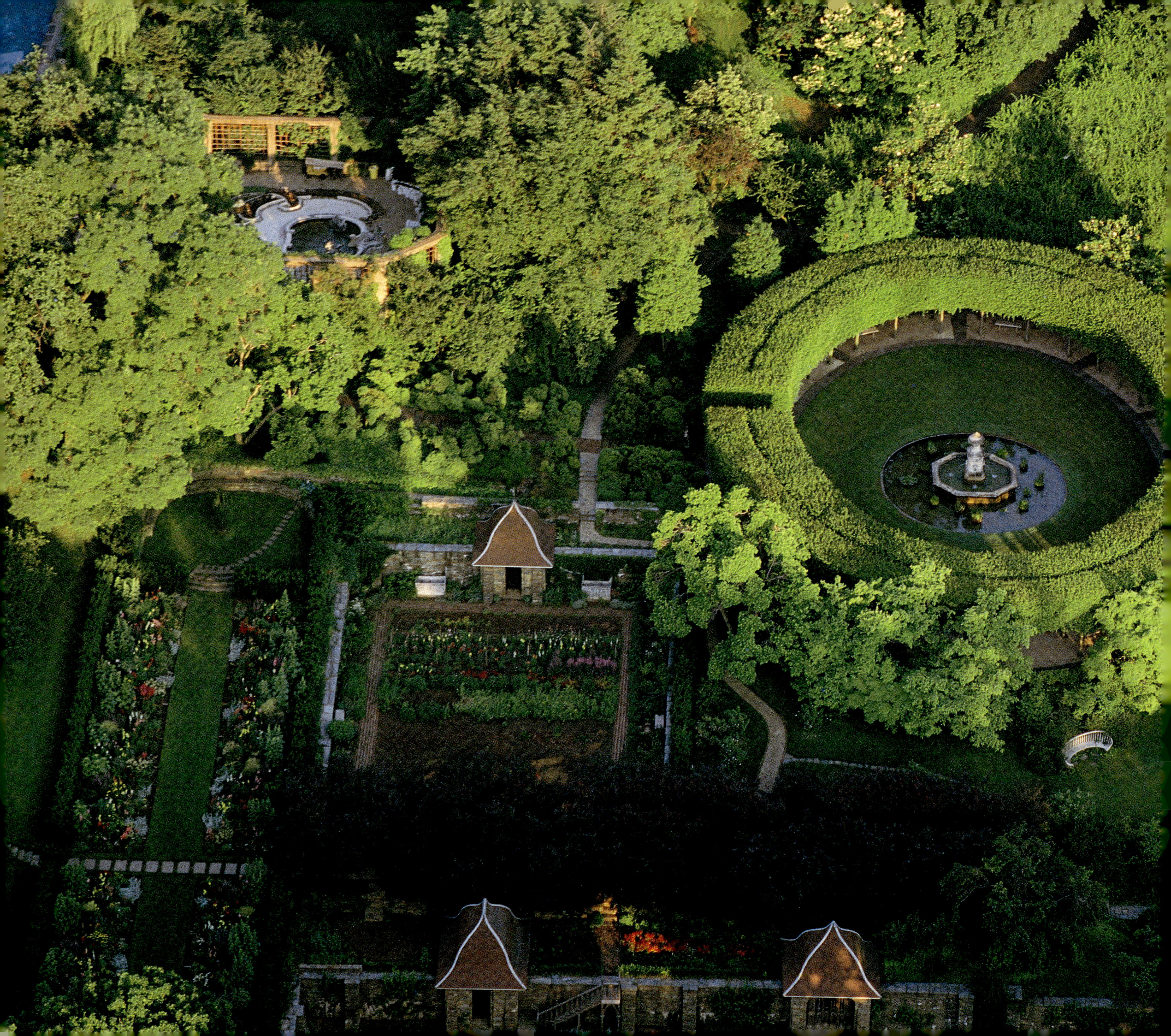

◀ Gardens of Dumbarton Oaks, Georgetown. Robert Woods Bliss and Mildred Barnes Bliss bought the Georgetown estate in 1920, later donating the bulk of it to Harvard University. Its 10-acre formal gardens were designed by Beatrix Farrand, who earlier had planned the Blisses' grounds in Bar Harbor, Maine. The circle of trees at the left are pleached—intertwined—to provide a walkway beneath them.

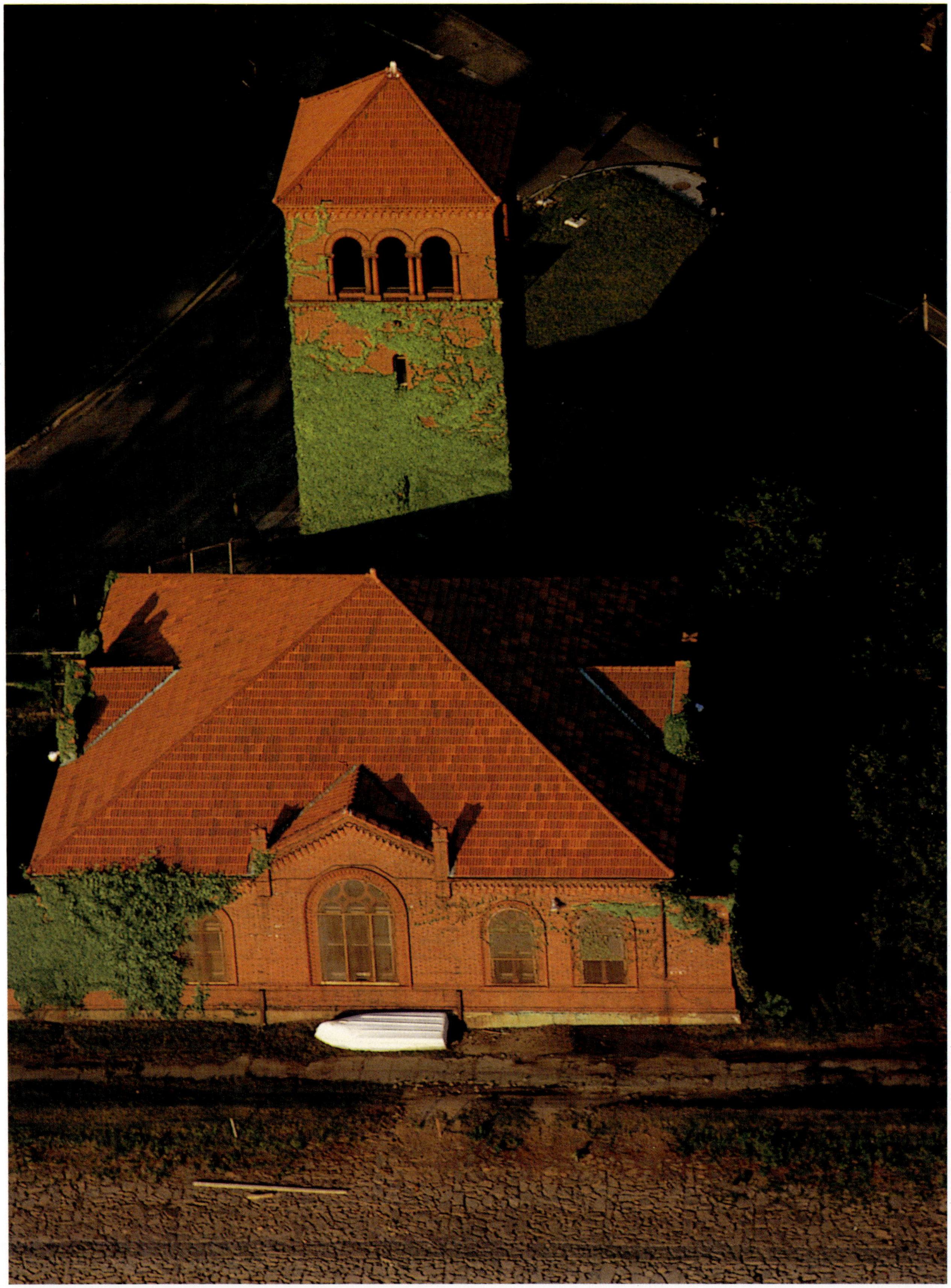

◀▲McMillan Reservoir and storage tanks. A well-disguised part of the District of Columbia's water system, the reservoir was built by the Army Corps of Engineers in the late 1800s. The water works houses a 160-foot shaft in its church-like tower. Built around the turn of the century, the now idle tanks once held sand for the water-system's underground filters. Donkey carts carried the sand from the tanks to the manhole covers in the background.

▲▶Washington Harbour and docking area, Georgetown. In an article in *The Washington Post*, Washington Harbour's architect, Arthur Cotton Moore, likened the complex's 23 separate facades to a "complicated recipe for a major dish," where "details such as salt, pepper, or lemon juice taken alone are obviously too much, but in a great bouillabaisse, it is the completed compound's taste from combined flavoring that is satisfying." Not everyone agreed. One critic, unhappy with its modern appearance, responded that the "Harbour refuses to acknowledge the historical context of Georgetown....It might as well have landed there from outer space."

39

▲Looking south along Sixteenth and Seventeenth Streets. In 1913 Congress officially changed the name of Sixteenth Street, seen here to the left of center, to the Avenue of the Presidents. The grand moniker survived only a year before Congress reversed its decision.

▶The White House. Begun in 1792 by Irish architect James Hoban, the original presidential mansion was modeled after the Duke of Leinster's house, meeting place of the Irish Parliament in Dublin. Its first occupants were John and Abigail Adams, who used the unfinished East Room to dry their laundry. Burned down in 1814 by the British, the mansion was rebuilt by Hoban in 1817. Until the administration of Theodore Roosevelt, the White House was generally referred to as the "President's Palace" or "President's House."

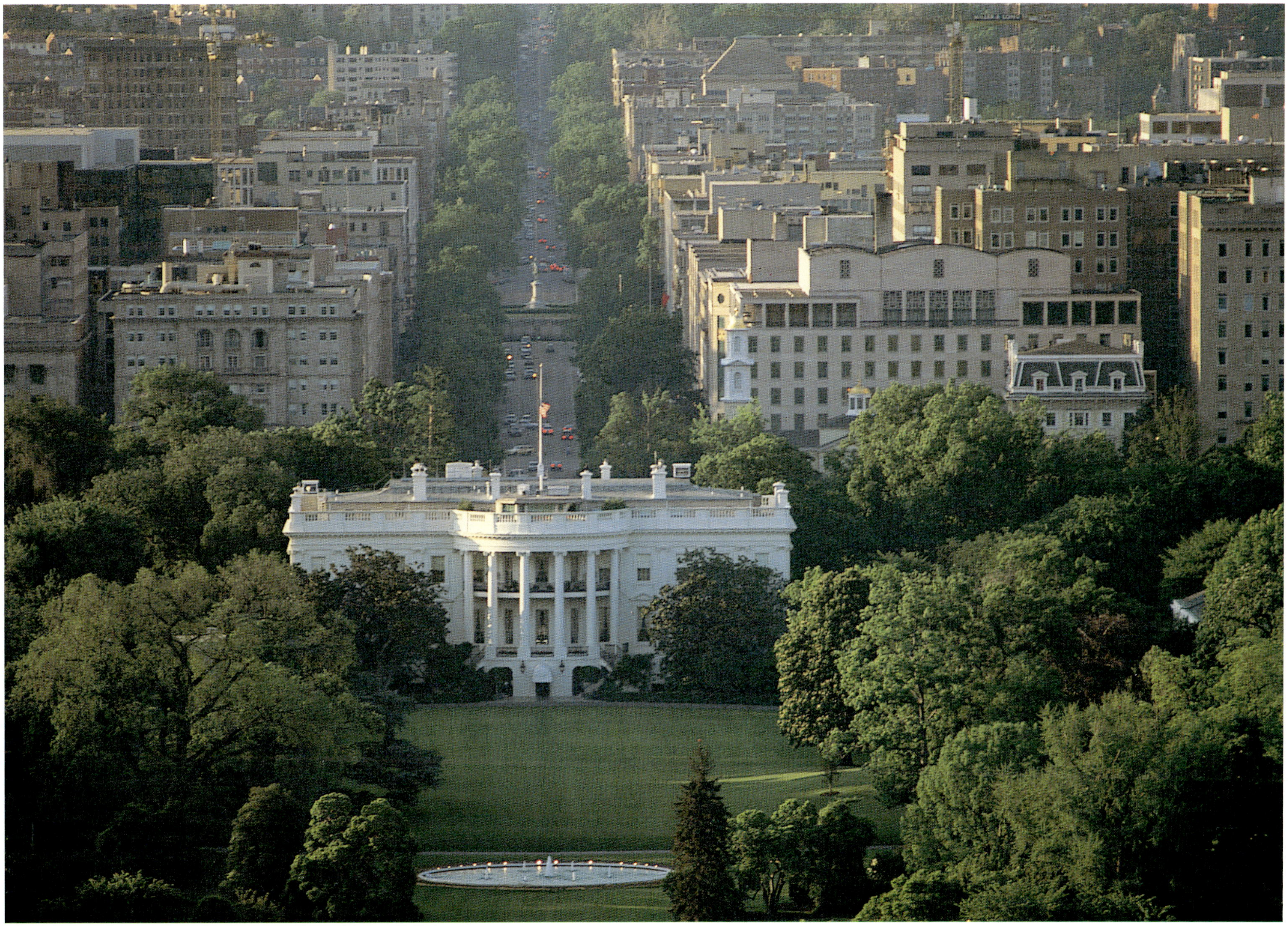

42

▲National Gallery of Art. Completed in 1941, the art gallery reflects the neo-classical architectural design that John Russell Pope deemed appropriate for the Federal City's public buildings. To the top of the photograph sits the National Air and Space Museum, here glowing an extra-terrestrial green. The eerie glow comes from interior "wall washes"—high-filter accent lights shining through the museum's tinted-glass walls. The museum opened in 1976.

◀Smithsonian Institution. Built in the 1850s, the "Castle" was designed by James Renwick. The institution's benefactor, James Smithson, died in 1829 without ever setting foot in America, but in 1904 his remains were brought to Washington and interred in the castle. The doughnut-shaped Hirshhorn Museum, top right, houses a collection of modern art. In the foreground are the pyramidal and domed tops of the Smithsonian's new underground museums, the Arthur M. Sackler Gallery and the National Museum of African Art.

▲ Old Executive Office Building. Originally called the State, War, and Navy Building when it was completed in 1888, the structure, with its 900 Doric columns and "wedding cake" facade, was for many years the largest office building in the world.

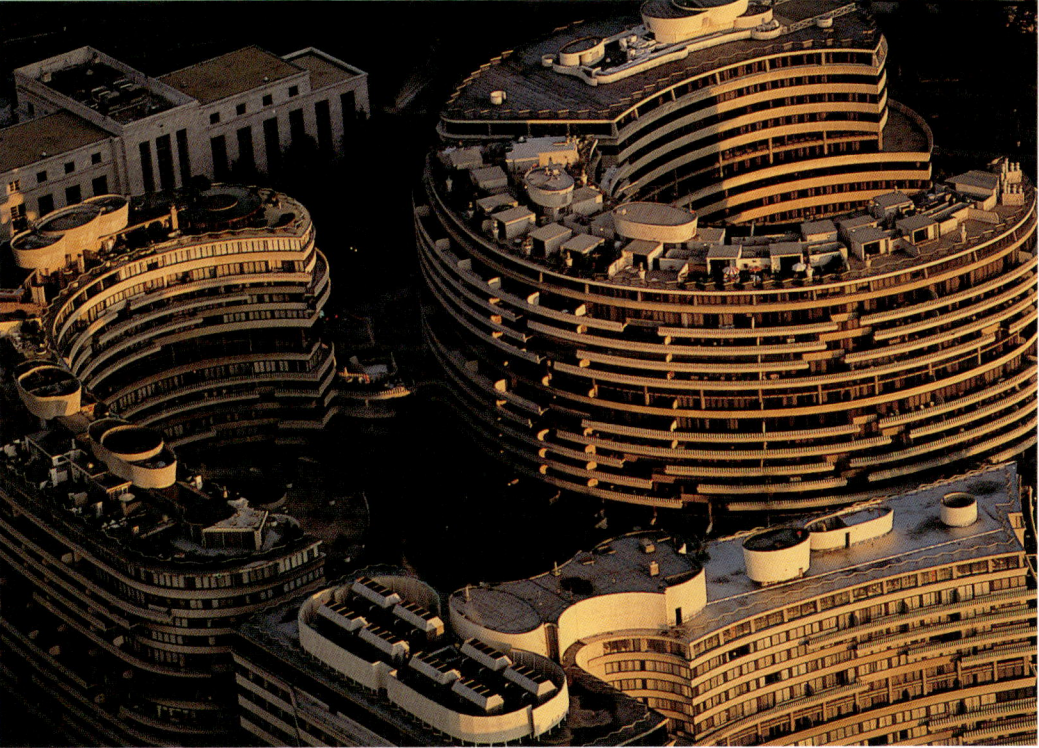

◀Governmental district. To the left can be seen the towered Post Office Pavilion; to the right, a federal office complex. Among the federal building's tenants are the Bureau of Alcohol, Tobacco, and Firearms and sections of the Justice Department.

◀Watergate. Easily recognizable because of its curvaceous design, the Watergate residential and commercial complex became famous on June 17, 1972, when five men armed with photographic and wire-tapping equipment were caught breaking into the Democratic National Committee headquarters located there. The facility got its name from 40 granite "Water Gate" steps that descend toward the Potomac River nearby.

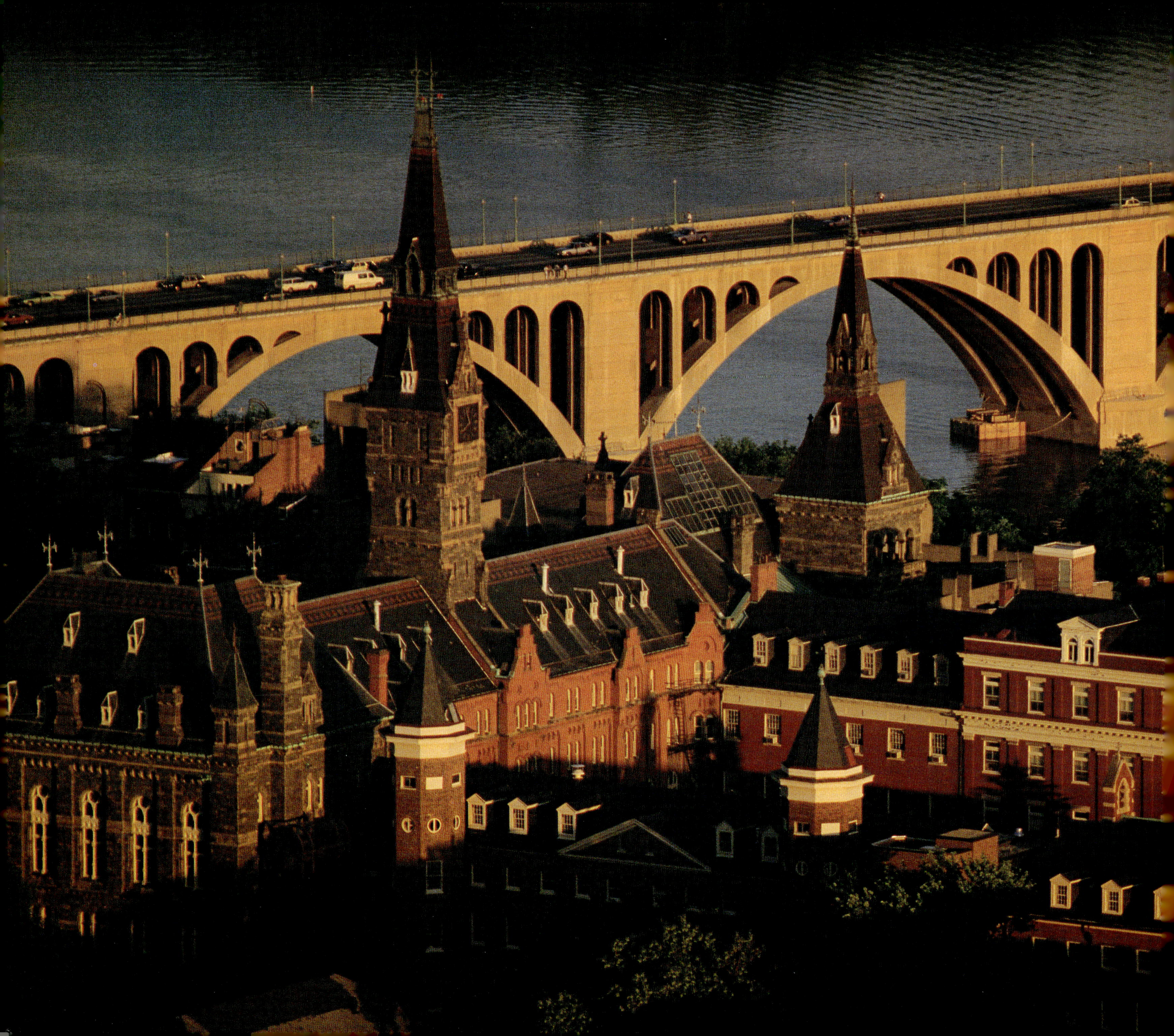

◀ Georgetown University. Founded by the Society of Jesuits in 1789 — the same year that the city of George Town was incorporated — Georgetown University is the oldest Roman Catholic college in the United States. John Carroll, America's first Catholic bishop, had considered establishing the school on what is now Capitol Hill but later decided the site was "too far in the country." In the background can be seen Key Bridge. Named for Francis Scott Key, it is one of three bridges in the district honoring songwriters. The others: the Duke Ellington and John Philip Sousa Bridges.

▲▶ Flying buttresses and *Gloria in Excelsis* tower, the Washington National Cathedral. The foundation stone for the cathedral, officially named the Cathedral Church of Saint Peter and Saint Paul, came from a quarry at Bethlehem and was laid in 1907 atop Mount St. Alban, often mistaken for the highest piece of ground in the region. Cradled in the four spires of the cathedral's 300-foot central tower are telecommunication antennae leased by the Motorola Corporation for use by District of Columbia police and others referred to generically as "government."

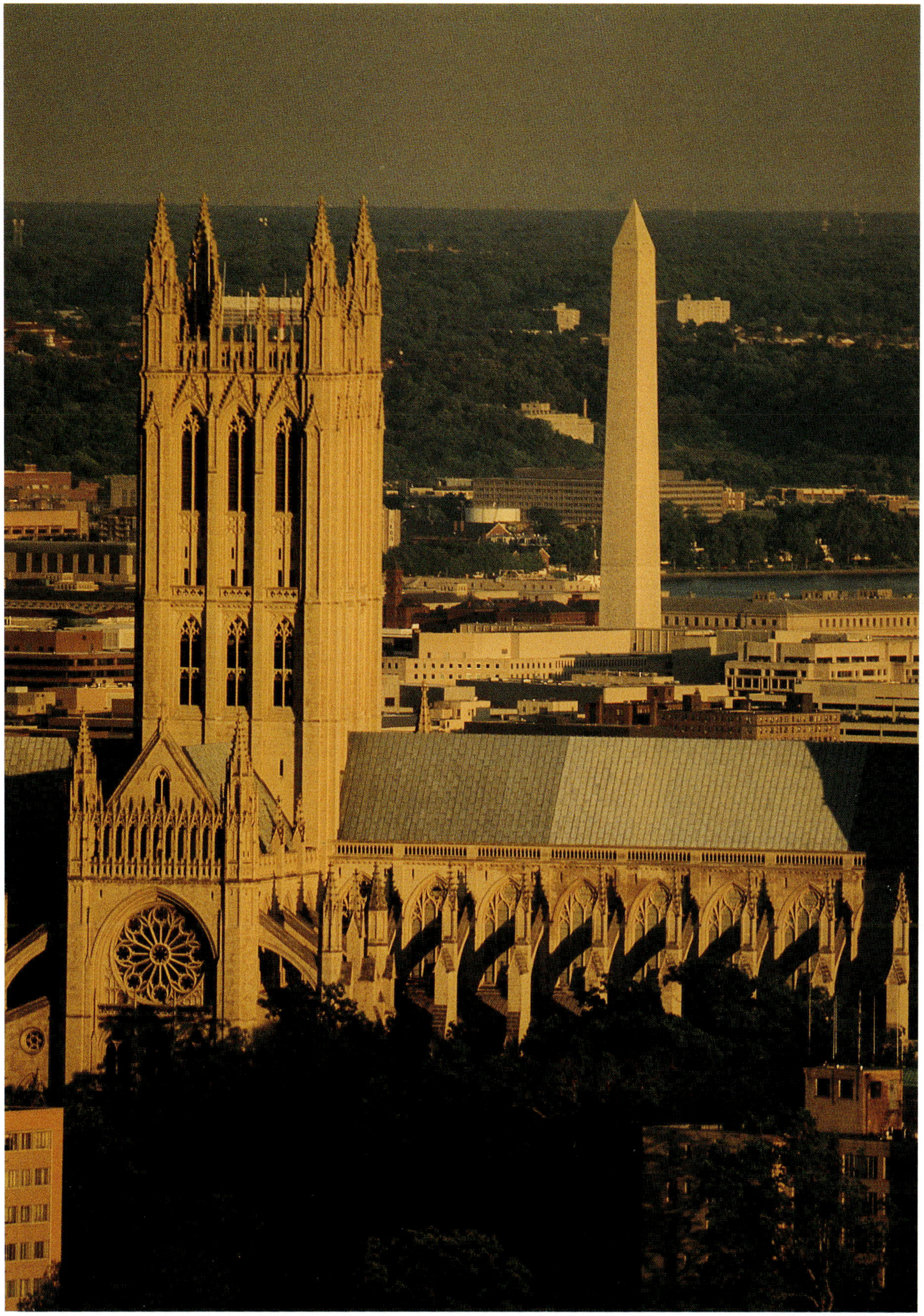

▲ John F. Kennedy Center for the Performing Arts. Edward Durell Stone was commissioned in 1959 to design a national cultural center, but the effort languished until after Kennedy's assassination in 1963. Today the finished complex houses an opera stage, concert hall, two theaters, and a cinema.

▲Washington Harbour. The large building to the rear of Washington Harbour is the General Services Administration's West Heating Plant, where oil and coal are burned to provide steam heat for the White House.

▶▶Marilyn Monroe mural and residential neighborhood, northwest Washington. The mural of the former Norma Jean Mortenson that is painted on Salon Roi, located at the intersection of Connecticut Avenue and Calvert Street, was a gift of the late hairdresser Charles Stinson to his friend Roi Barnard. The artist was John Bailey.

53

▲ Naval Observatory and Vice President's mansion. Located in a 73-acre park near the British Embassy on Massachusetts Avenue, the mansion was built at the turn of the century for the superintendent of the observatory. In 1928 it became the residence of the Chief of Naval Operations and, in 1974, the home of Vice Presidents. Its first vice-presidential occupants were the Walter Mondales. Official United States time is kept at the observatory by a cesium-beam atomic clock, accurate to within one-ten-billionth of a second per day.

▲Ethel Kennedy's Hickory Hill estate in McLean, Virginia. The main house, seen here to the right, was built on the foundations of an earlier structure that had been destroyed by fire during the Civil War. Robert Jackson, Supreme Court Justice from 1941 to 1954, was one of Hickory Hill's earlier owners.

◀Footbridge to Roosevelt Island. Once known as Analostan, the Potomac River island was the site of the manor home of John Mason, whose father George wrote the Virginia Declaration of Rights, the forerunner of the Constitution's Bill of Rights.

▶Looking south down Wisconsin Avenue in Georgetown. Once the ancient village of Tohoga, Georgetown was founded by a tribe of Indians at the fall line of the Potomac River. The golden dome of Riggs National Bank, located at the corner of M Street and Wisconsin Avenue, rises above the community's many restaurants, shops, and nightclubs.

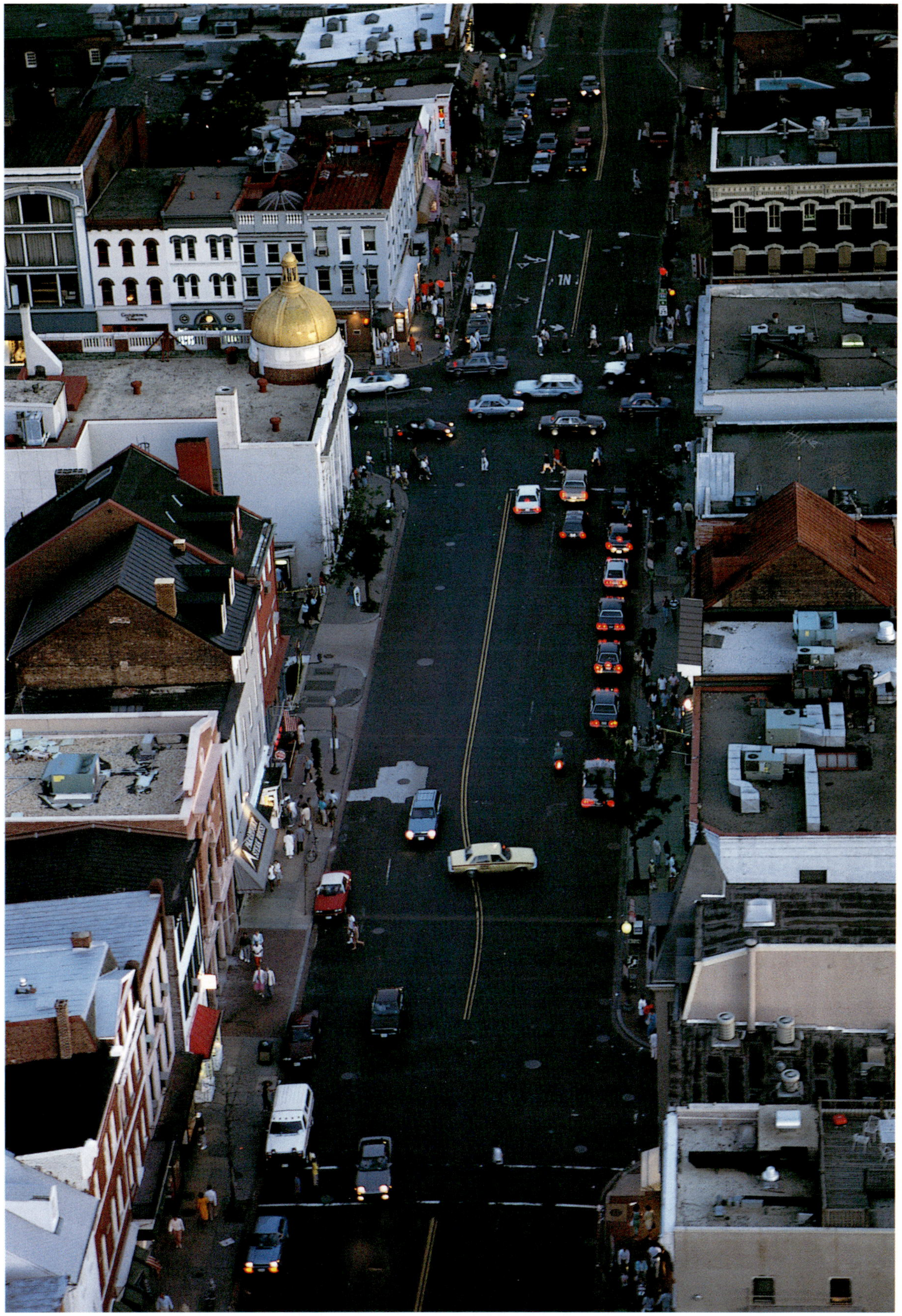

▲ Business district in northeast Washington.

▶National Shrine of the Immaculate Conception, Catholic University of America. The shrine, 150 yards long and 80 yards wide at the transept, is the largest Roman Catholic church in the United States and the seventh largest in the world. Its tower houses a 56-bell carillon.

▶▶Islamic Center. Opened in 1957, the mosque was funded by the 29 Moslem nations that then had diplomatic representation in the nation's capital. It is turned away from Massachusetts Avenue so that it will face towards Mecca. Islamic Center officials estimate there are about 70,000 Moslems in the Washington area.

▲ Pentagon. With nearly four million square feet of interior space — three times the floor space of the Empire State Building in New York City — the Pentagon is the world's largest office building. A helicopter pad sits in the foreground.

▲ Central Intelligence Agency in Langley, Virginia. The grid of steel on the new 1.1-million-square-foot addition is encased by a curtain of glass, most likely to form successive layers of security. The cost of the building remains classified.

▶ The Yard at Howard University. Chartered by Congress in 1867 and named for General Oliver Howard, onetime chief of the Freedman's Bureau and the school's first president, Howard is the alma mater of many famous black leaders, including Supreme Court Justice Thurgood Marshall, Atlanta Mayor Andrew Young, and eminent psychologist Kenneth Clark. More than 11,000 students attend Howard each year.

▲ Gallaudet University. Founded in 1857 by Amos Kendall as the Columbia Institution, Gallaudet comprises a student body of deaf men and women. Kendall, postmaster general under former president Andrew Jackson, was once the guardian of five deaf students, and his Kendall Green estate off northeast Florida Avenue now houses the college's main campus. Its grounds were designed in 1866 by Frederick Law Olmstead. Gallaudet takes its name from the school's first superintendent.

▶Pennsylvania Avenue. When planning the nation's capital two centuries ago, Pierre Charles L'Enfant envisioned a "Grand Avenue connecting both the palace and the federal house" to be created from a footpath through trees and bushes beside the marshy reaches of Tiber Creek. The federal house—the Capitol—can be seen at top right.

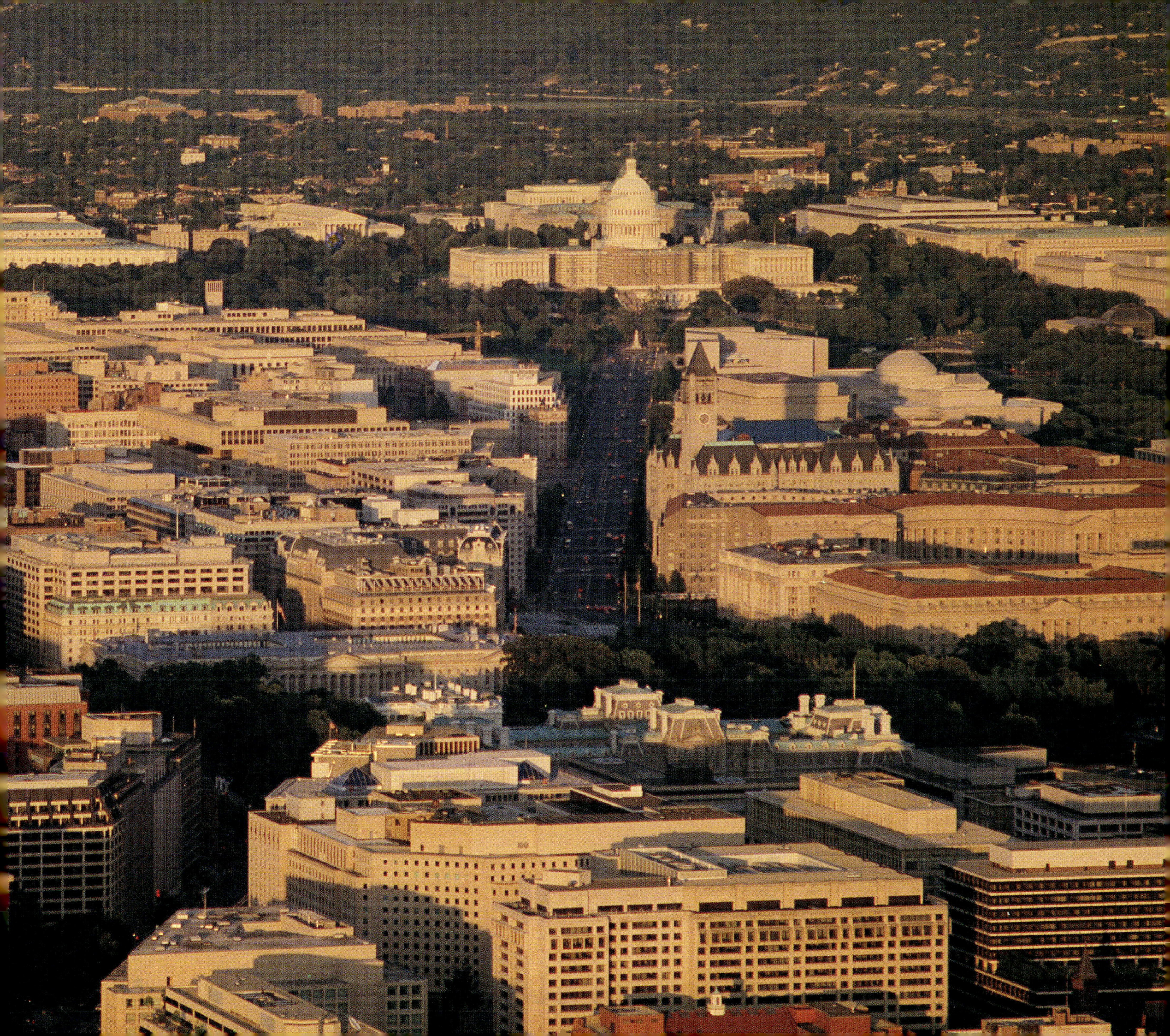

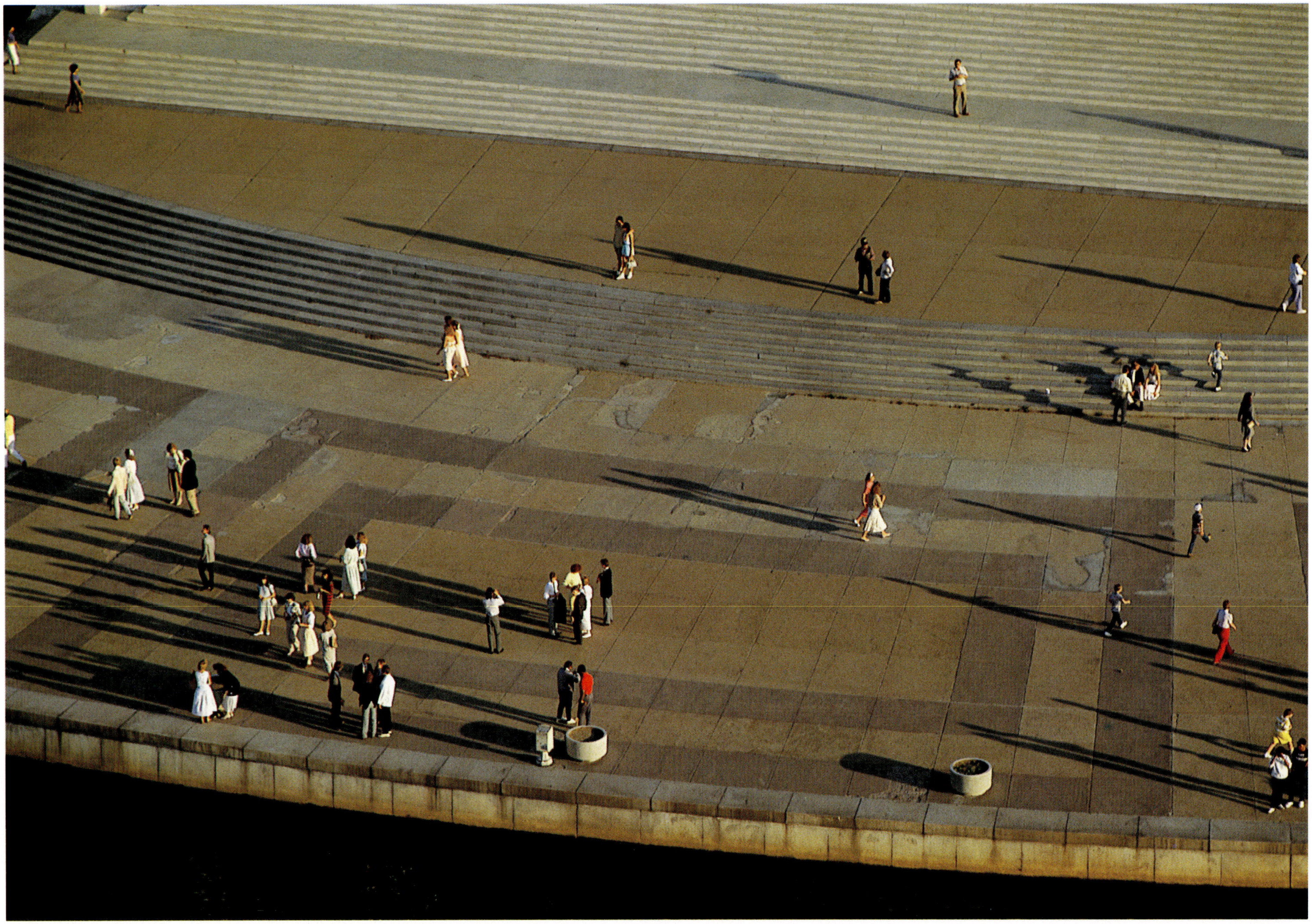

▲◀"The Awakening" and the Jefferson Memorial. Located on Hains Point, just off the Washington Channel and the Potomac River, the aluminum sculpture is the work of Seward Johnson Jr., who once said that "combat is delicious. It's a wonderful way to sort out the truth."

68

▲A sculler gliding on the Potomac River. Crew races held in Washington usually begin at Three Sisters Rocks in front of the Potomac Boat Club and finish 2,000 meters later in front of the Kennedy Center for Performing Arts.

◀Georgetown Reservoir Gate House. The castle-like structure, built at the turn of the century, contains gates that control the flow of water to the McMillan Reservoir. Its design derives from the emblem of its builders, the Army Corps of Engineers.

▶ Georgetown and Rosslyn, Virginia, connected by Key Bridge. As recently as four decades ago, Rosslyn was routinely described in guides to the capital as a "small industrial town." Today it is a mass of high-rise offices. Centered in the Potomac River is Theodore Roosevelt Island, accessible only by boat or footbridge.

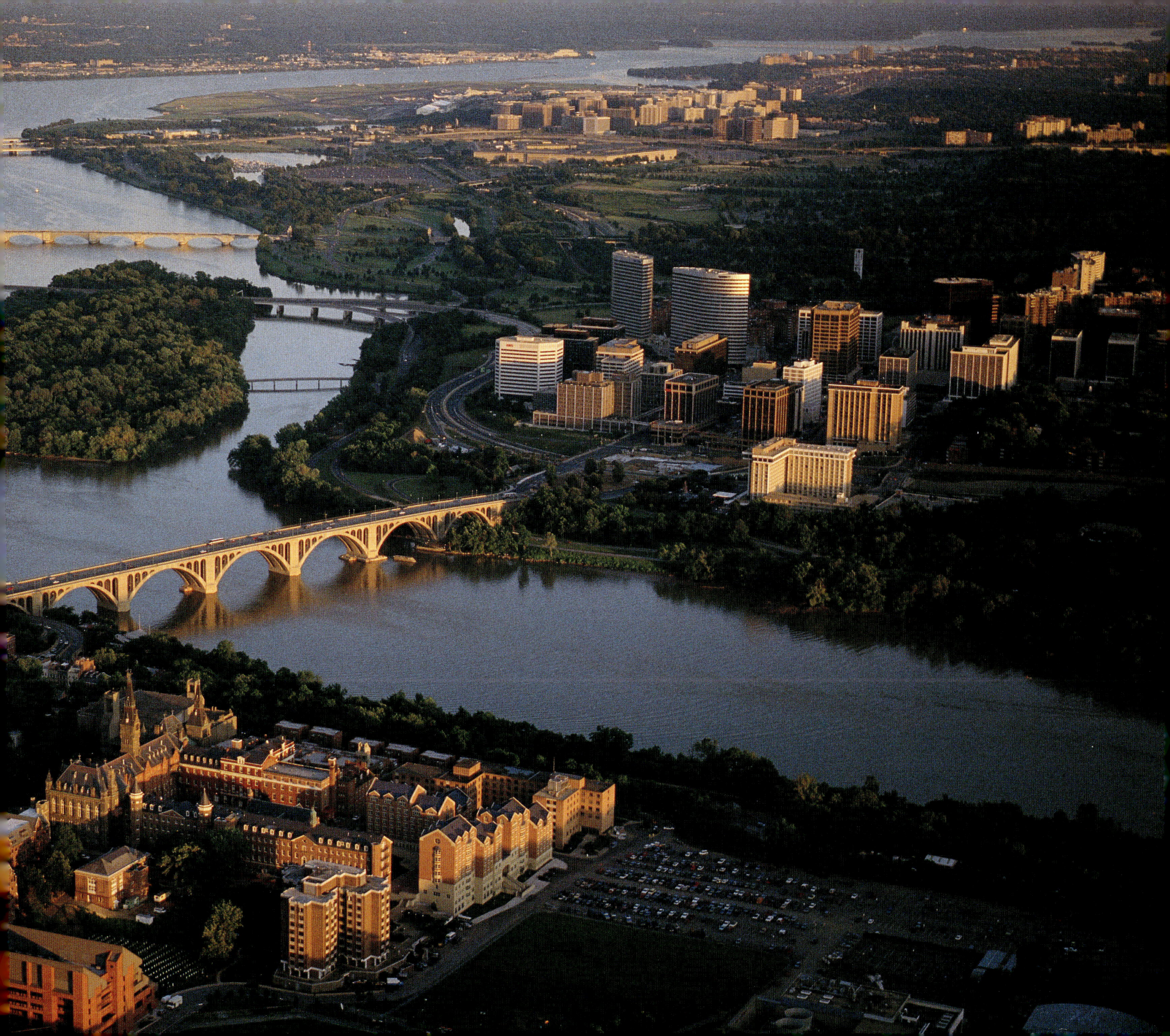

▲ *Spirit of Mt. Vernon*. Making one of its twice daily runs between Pier 4 on the Washington Channel and George Washington's home at Mount Vernon, the 110-foot ship can transport as many as 360 passengers.

▶ Old Towne Alexandria, Virginia. In 1669 Robert Howsen received a grant for 6,000 acres of land "on the freshes of the Potomac." The next year, the grant was purchased by Captain John Alexander. Named after the captain, Alexandria was laid out in 1791 and originally considered part of the borders of the District of Columbia. More than a half century later, angry that all the public buildings had been raised on the Maryland side of the river, Virginians took Alexandria back in an early act of secession. Today Alexandria contains over a thousand structures predating the twentieth century.

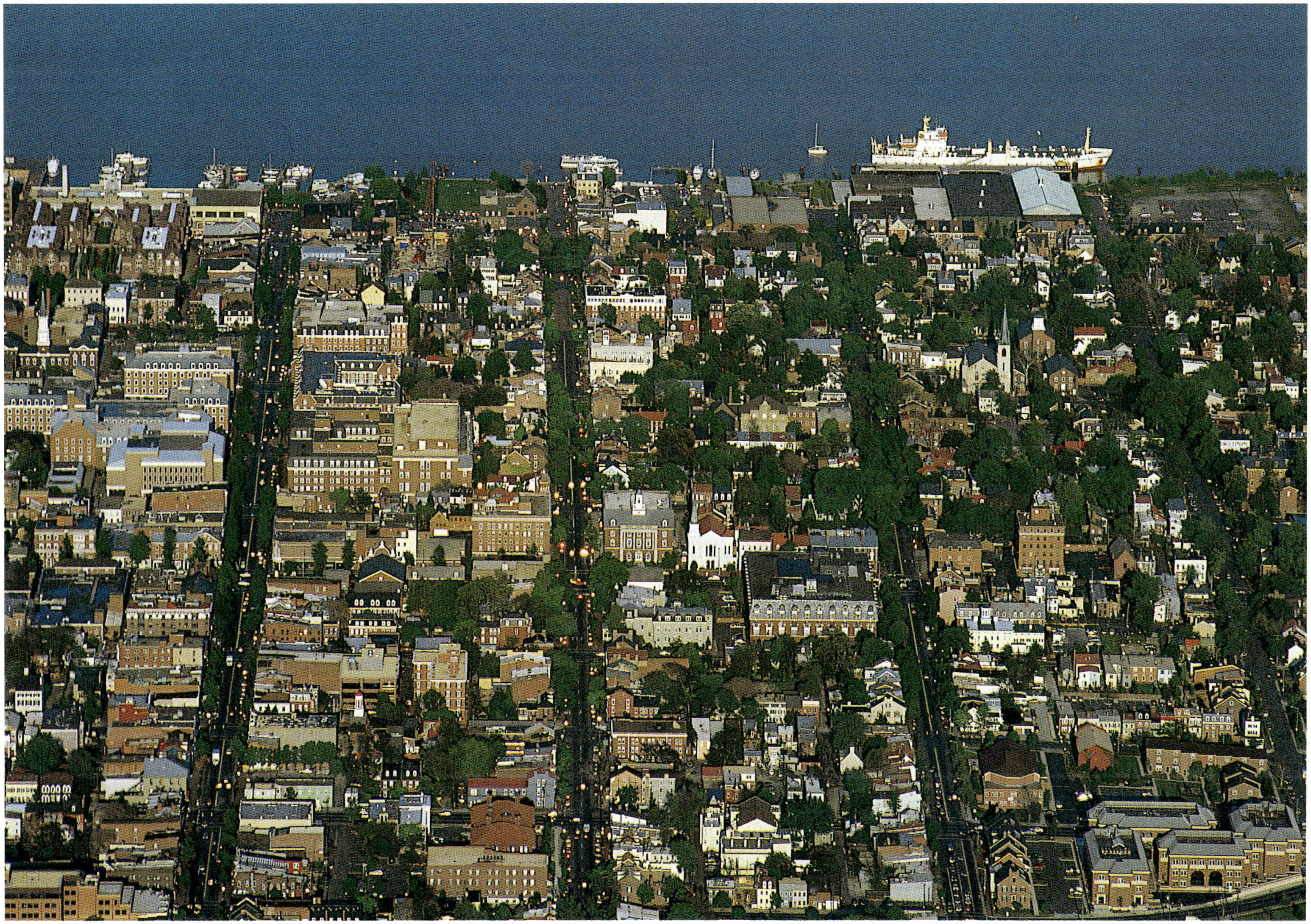

▶ Lincoln Park. In 1876, nearly half a century before Congress could cause a memorial to be raised in honor of Abraham Lincoln, Thomas Ball's Emancipation Monument was unveiled at Lincoln Park. It was paid for by freed slaves. The park also contains a more recent bronze statue of black educator Mary McLeod Bethune.

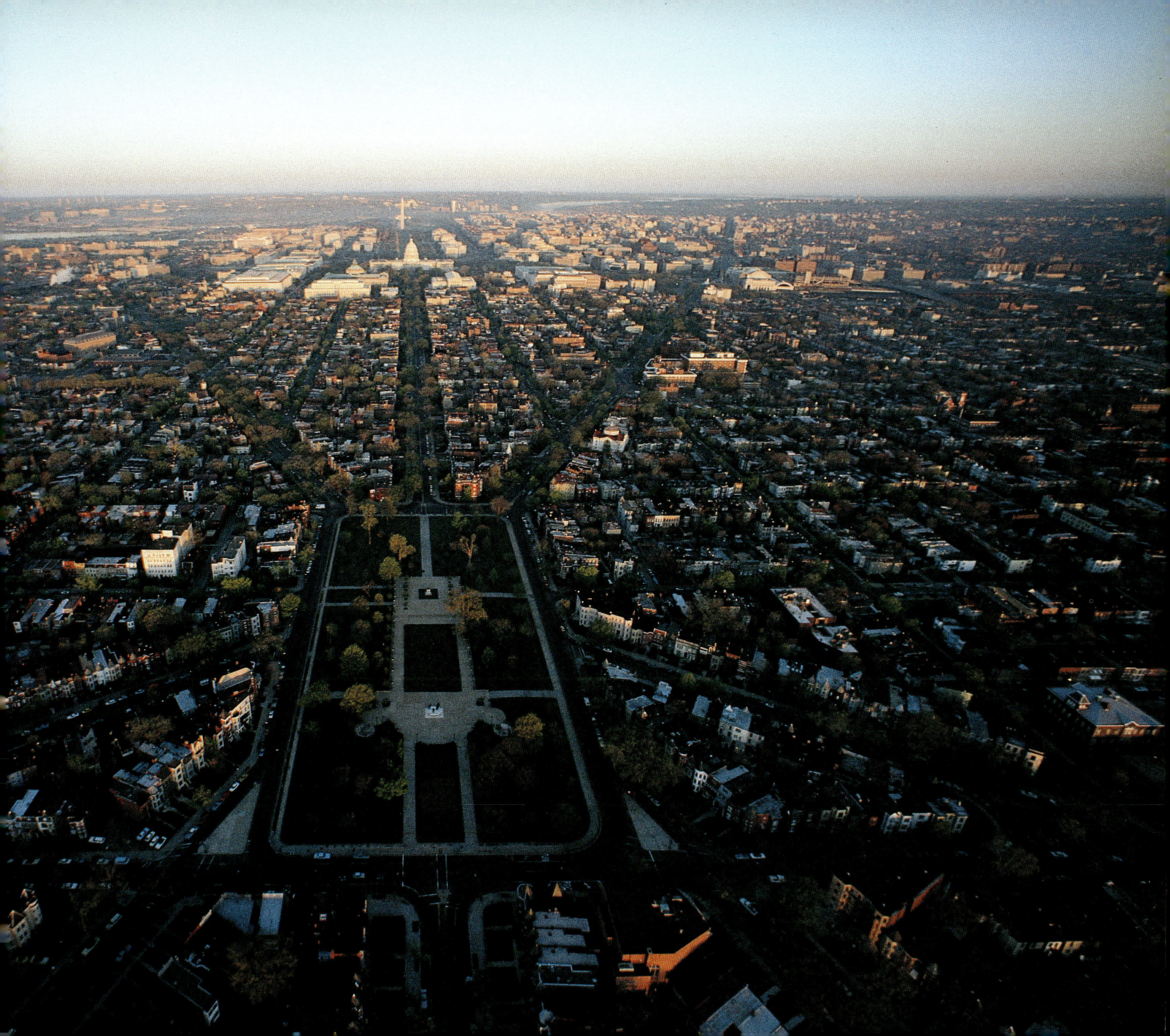

▲▶ Washington National Airport and the TWA Terminal. Built on dredged land at a site once known as Gravelly Point, the $12.5-million airport was dedicated in September 1940. The first official landing there was made by an airplane owned by the Civil Aeronautics Board, followed by planes from the three airlines that first served the airport—American, Eastern, and Pennsylvania-Central.

77

▶Memorial Bridge, West Potomac Park, the Tidal Basin, and the Jefferson Memorial as seen from above Arlington, Virginia. The Tidal Basin is more than a scenic adjunct to the Federal City. Floodgates located where it meets the Potomac River are used to clear debris accumulated in the still waters of Washington Channel harbor. As is much of the District of Columbia south of the White House, both East and West Potomac Parks are built on reclaimed land. "Valor," the equestrian statue on the north terminus of Memorial Bridge, was cast in Florence, Italy, in 1950 — a gift from the people of that country.

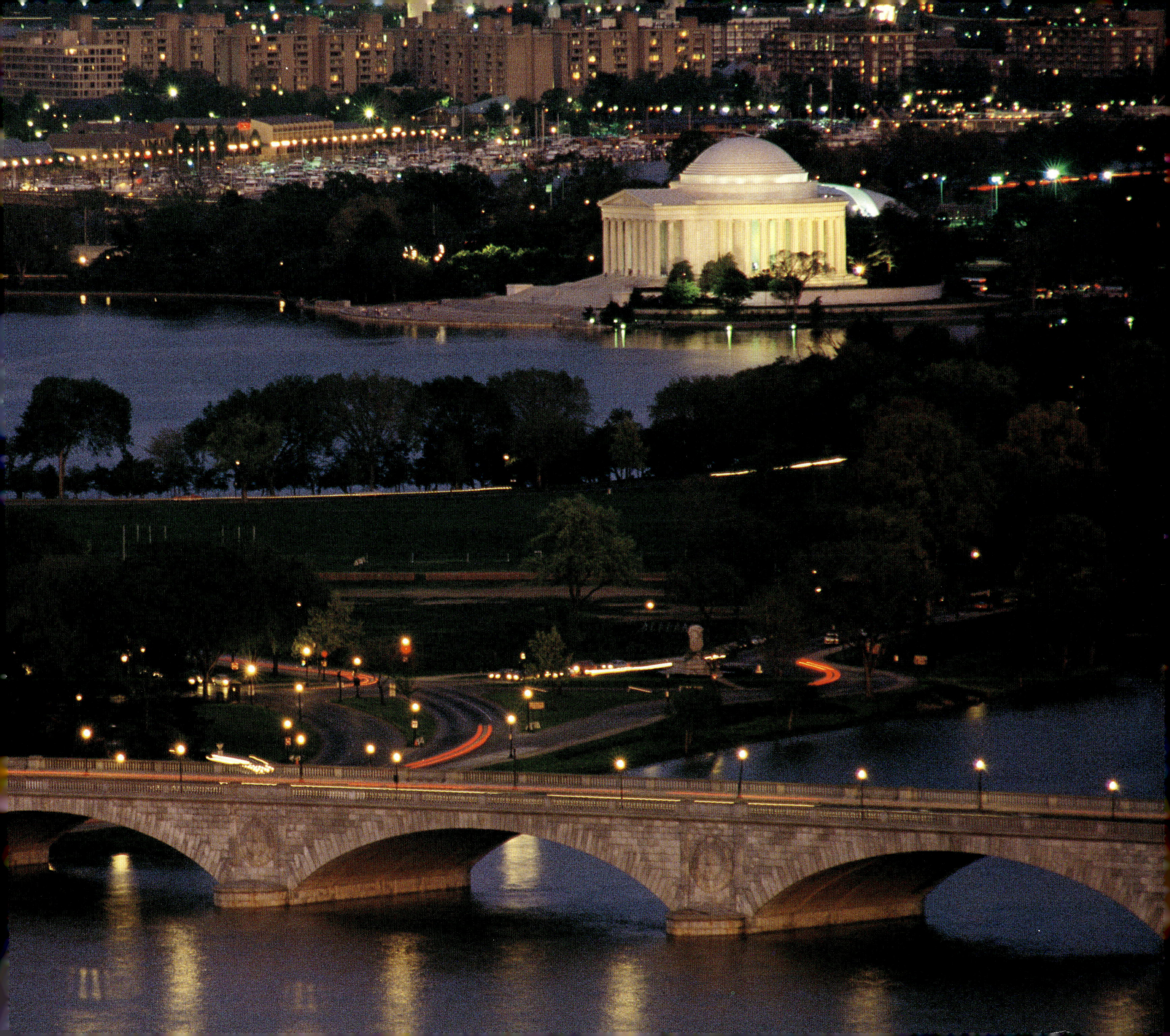

BEYOND THE BELTWAY

▶ Mormon Temple in Kensington, Maryland. Plated in gold, the Angel Moroni stands atop the golden spires of the marble temple and overlooks Interstate 495 — the "Beltway" — sixteen stories below. The Church of Jesus Christ of the Latter-Day Saints teaches that Moroni was the last record keeper of a lost race of Americans annihilated in 421 A.D. It was Moroni who 14 centuries later delivered to Joseph Smith the plates from which the Book of Mormon was translated. In keeping with church practice, the temple is closed to non-Mormons.

81

▲Gunston Hall Plantation near Lorton, Virginia. Built by George Mason in 1755, the plantation now sits on 550 acres of the original 5,000-acre estate. Rescued by the Garden Club of Virginia in the 1950s, its gardens are planted in their original pattern—a French *parterre* sectioned into geometric designs and outlined, in this case, by boxwoods. The central *allee* of boxwoods was planted by Mason himself.

▶Bethesda Country Club, Montgomery County, Maryland. Bethesda takes its name from a pool in Jerusalem that, according to biblical verse John 5:2-9, has miraculous healing powers.

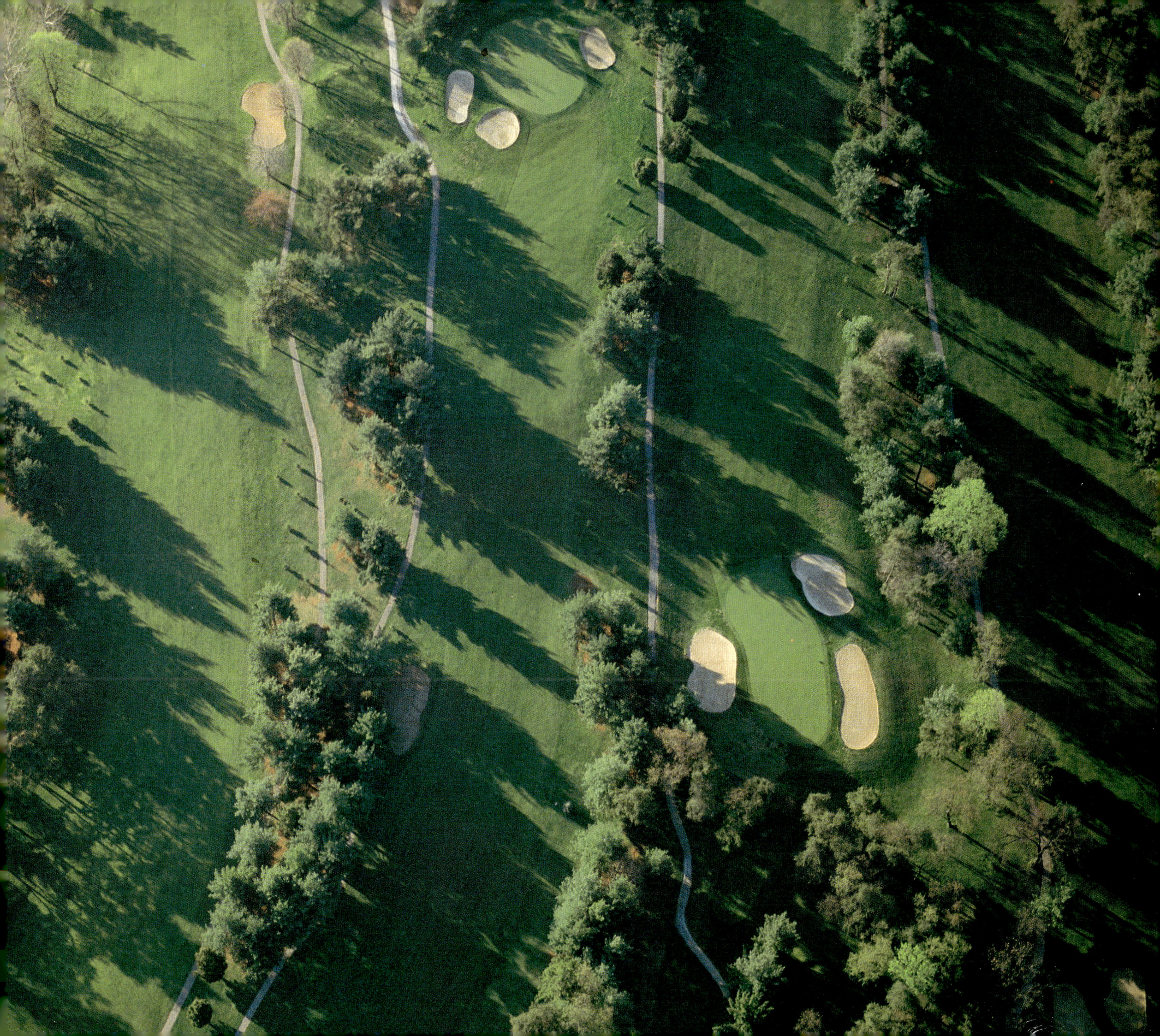

▲Townhouses in Reston, Virginia. New York developer Robert E. Simon, whose initials live on in the town's name, began the planned community on 7,400 acres once owned primarily by the Bowman family of bourbon distillery fame. Simon, in turn, sold the undeveloped land to Gulf Oil. Today, what remains undeveloped is owned by a division of Mobil Oil. First occupied in 1964, Reston should be completely filled by the mid-1990s with a population of about 62,000. "Planned community" is not a light-hearted phrase at Reston. Its Design Review Board has even decreed that basketball backboards be painted a flat gray-brown known locally as "Reston brown."

▲ Wolf Trap Farm Park in Northern Virginia. America's only national park for the performing arts, Wolf Trap faced extinction in 1982 when fire destroyed the complex's main stage, the Filene Center. Today's rebuilt Filene Center seats 3,766, with another 3,000 lawn seats available for opera, ballet, and on this June night, the Neville Brothers, Buckwheat Zydeco, and Dr. John. The park opened in 1971 on land donated by Catherine Filene Shouse.

▲Neighborhood baseball diamonds. Ever since the Washington Senators played their last game in 1971, Washingtonians have been without a major league baseball team. Today, the only professional baseball game held in the district is an exhibition game between an American League team and a National League team, played at Robert F. Kennedy Stadium on the Sunday preceding the regular major league season opener.

▶Columbia, Maryland. Begun in 1967 by developer James Rouse on a huge patch of farmland in Howard County, Columbia is quite possibly the nation's most famous planned community. Shown here are the Tides Fall townhouses on man-made Wilde Lake. Located halfway between Washington and Baltimore, Columbia is home to some 70,000 residents and about 2,000 businesses.

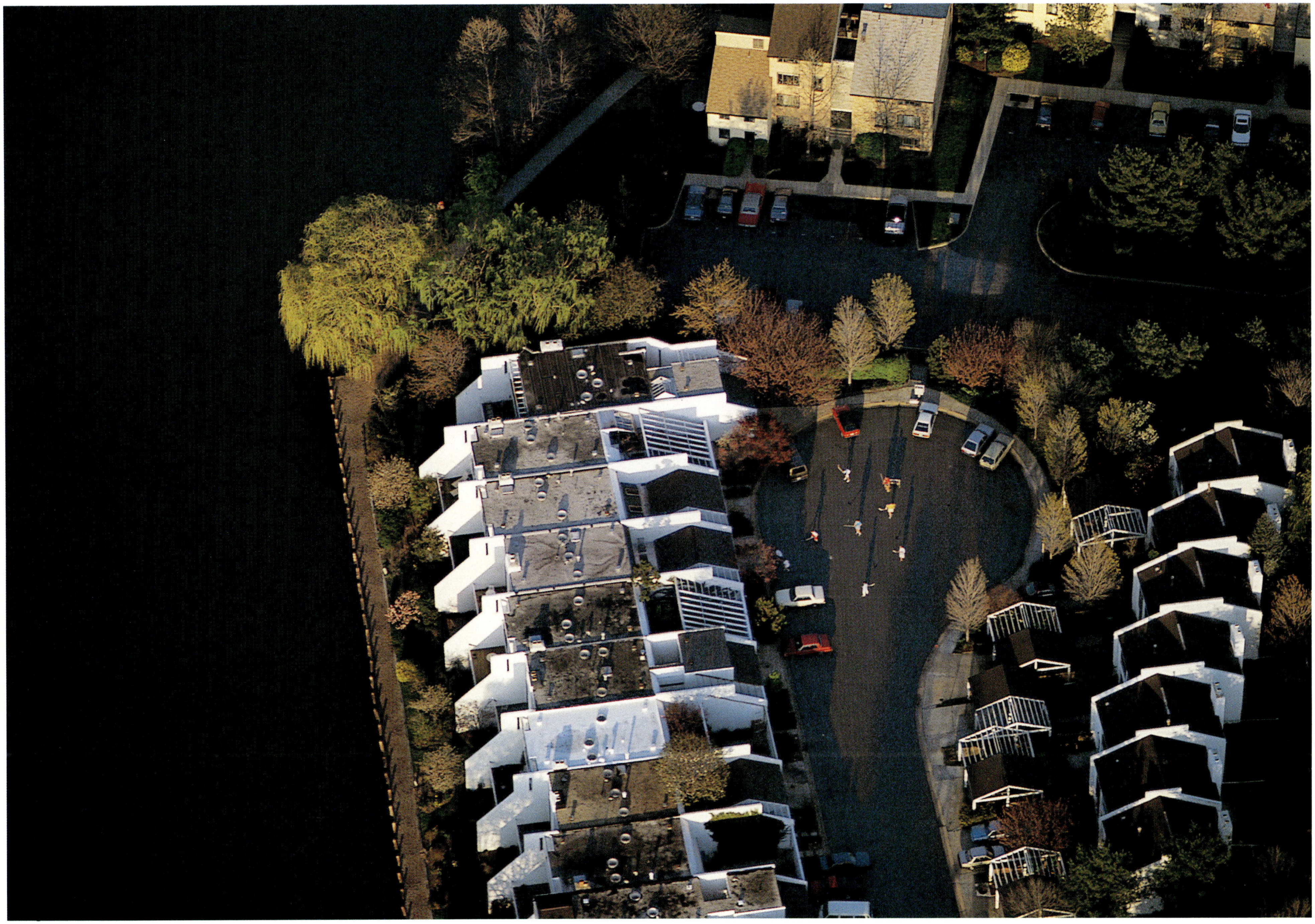

▶ Interstate 270 in Maryland. Constructed a few miles west of the old Frederick Road in order to connect Interstate 495 with Interstate 70 and other points west and north, Interstate 270 has given the one-time farmlands of Montgomery County a new crop — low-rise office complexes. Frederick County, located at Interstate 270's northern end, has doubled in population since the highway opened.

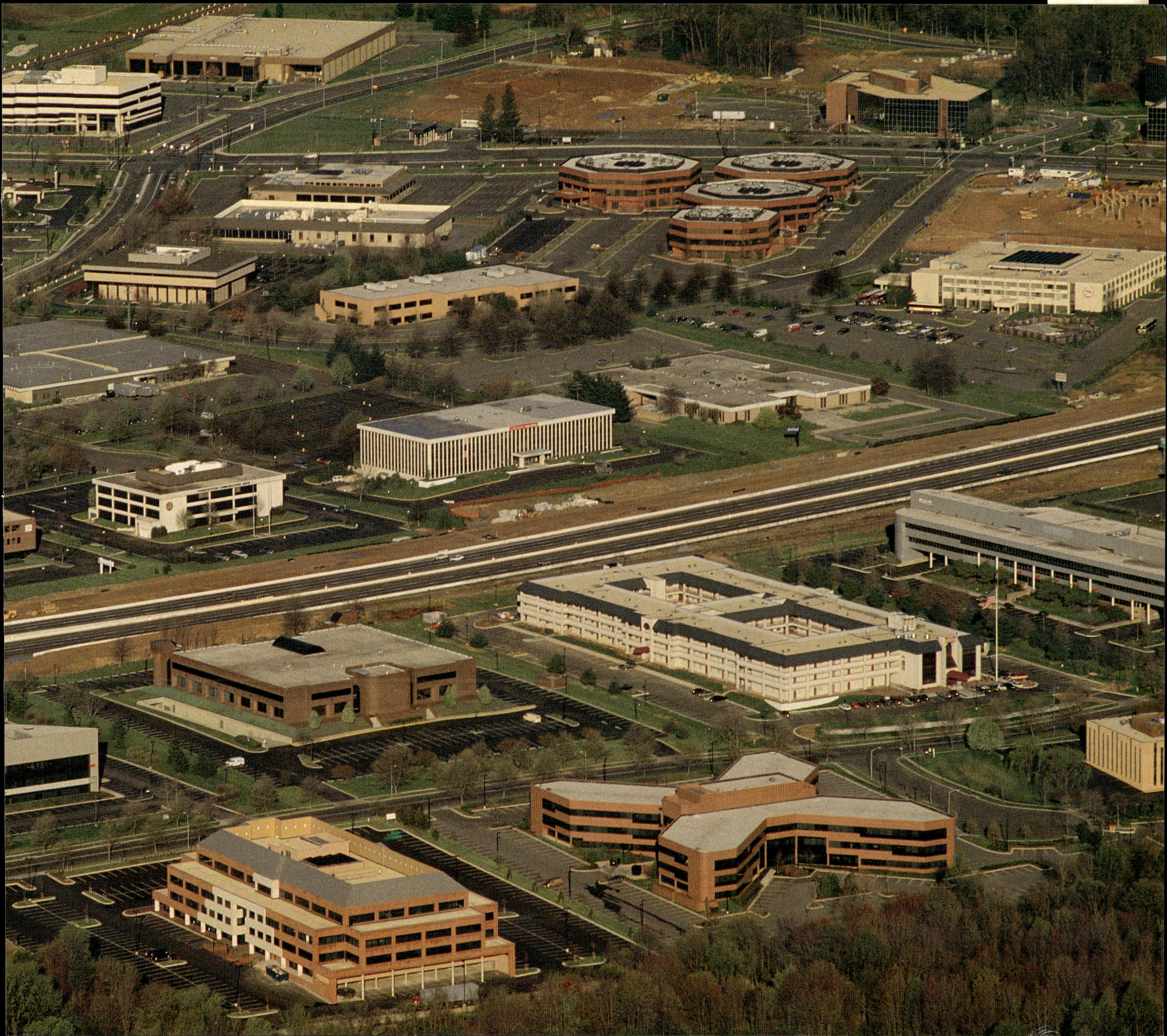

▲Interstate 395 in Virginia. Every day at rush hour some 20,000 cars pass this knotted interchange in varying states of confusion and frustration.

▶Fair Oaks Mall in Fairfax, Virginia. Built on the site of an old nine-hole golf course, the mall opened in July 1980. With 216 stores and 1.4 million square feet of floor space on two enclosed levels, the 119-acre plot is one of the area's largest shopping complexes.

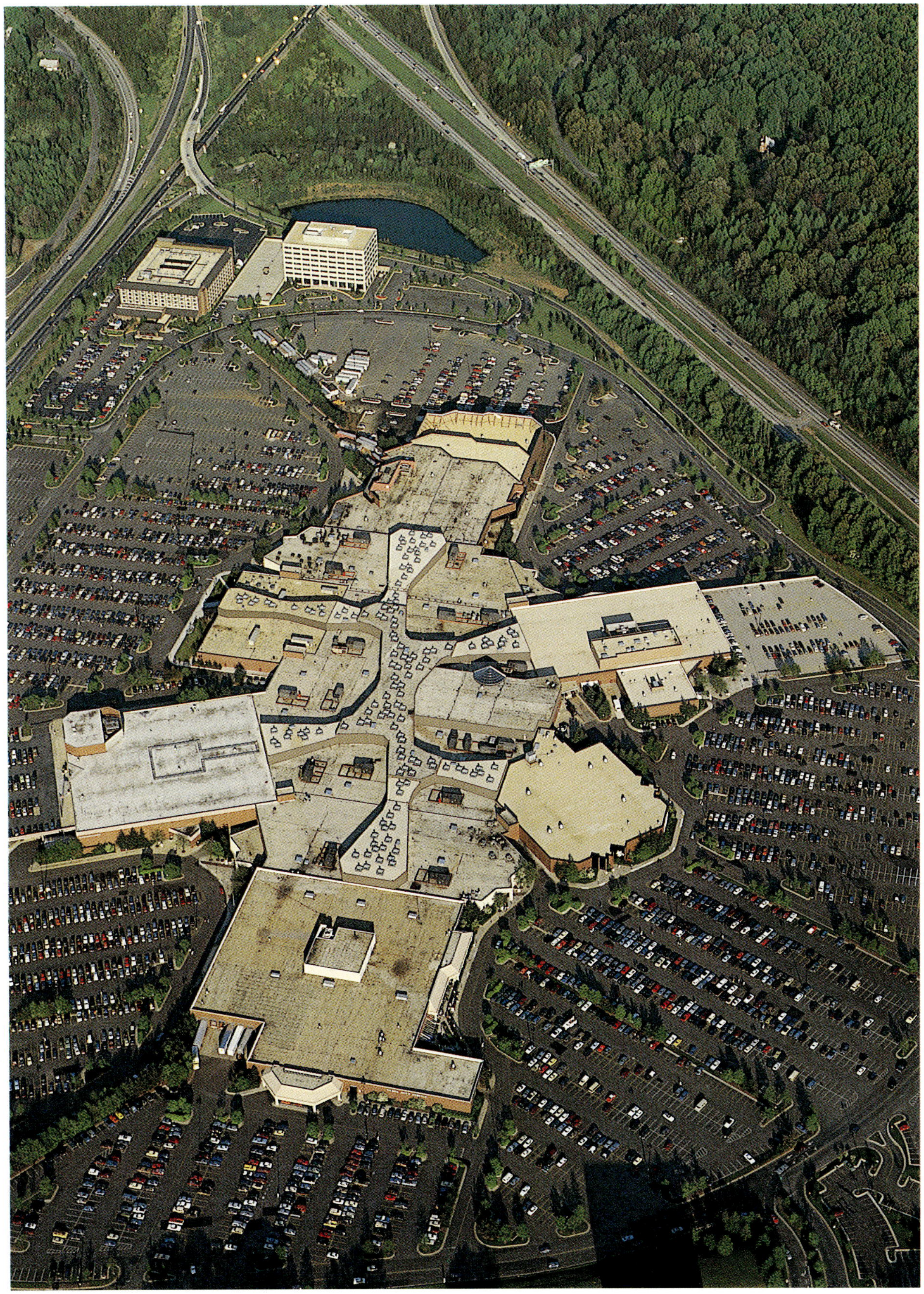

▲National Geographic Society Membership Center in Gaithersburg, Maryland. Opened two decades ago, the center was patterned after Edward Durell Stone's building for the National Geographic Society in downtown Washington. A small lake that existed on the 490-acre tract was reconfigured to provide the wet front yard. About 400 million pieces of mail a year are generated by this center, roughly one for every 13 people on the face of the planet.

▲Mobil Oil's corporate headquarters in Fairfax County, Virginia. Mobil's marketing and refining divisions moved into their new headquarters in 1980. The rear section, here under construction, will mirror the earlier structure.

▲▶ Xerox International Center for Training and Management Development near Leesburg, Virginia. Designed by the Vincent C. Kling Partnership, the 1.2-million-square-foot center sits on 2,265 acres of rolling countryside. Self-contained, the training facility, which opened in June 1974, includes dining areas, sales and service classrooms, and a fitness and recreation center. About a third of the year, it is leased to other corporations. A close-up view shows some of the 930 residence rooms.

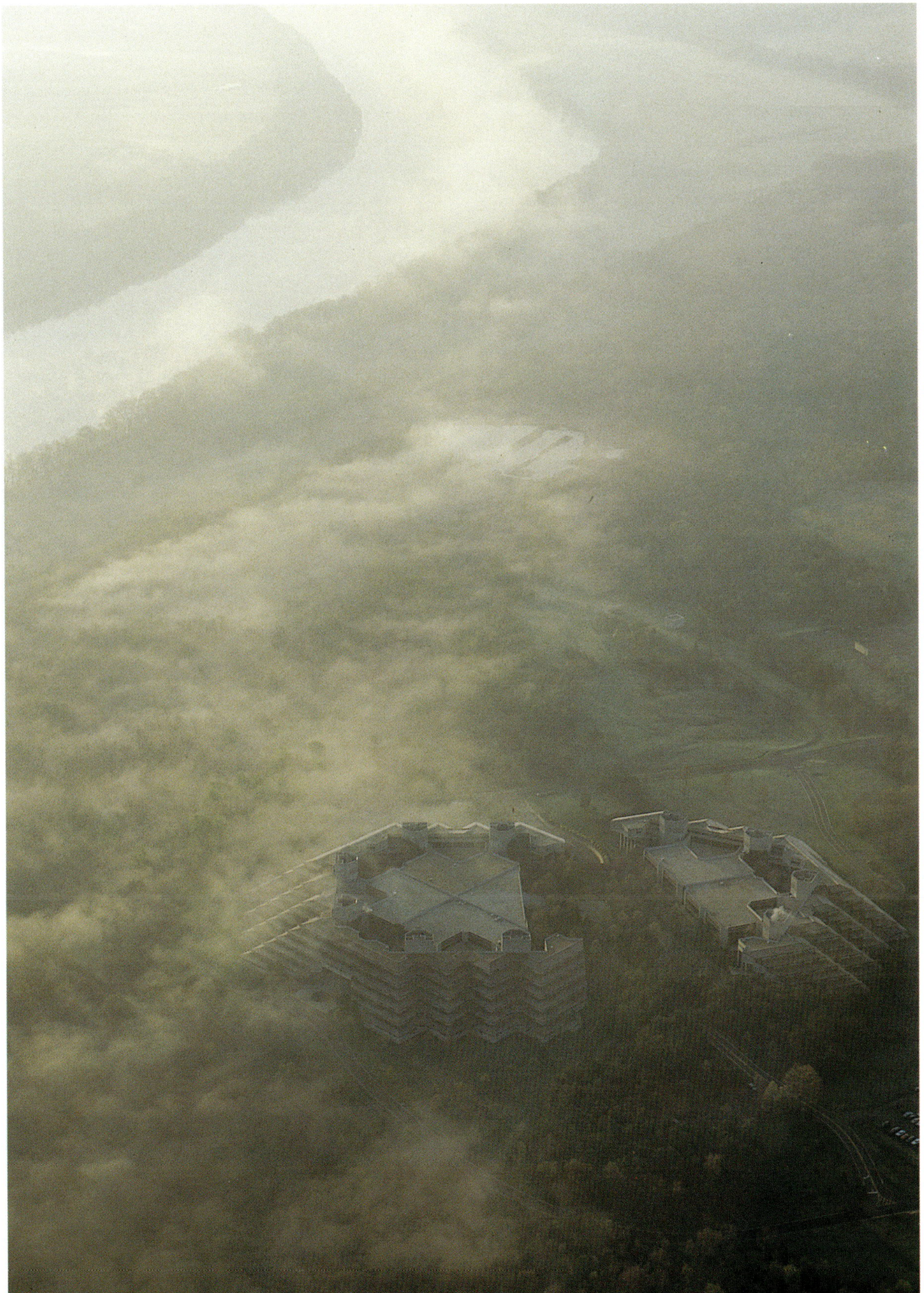

▶▶Dulles International Airport in Northern Virginia. Named for John Foster Dulles, Secretary of State during both Eisenhower administrations, the airport features a 600-foot-long terminal building designed by Eero Saarinen. Saarinen's plans provide for future expansion of the terminal along the same aesthetic lines to 1,200 feet. He died in 1961, a year before the airport opened. Dulles is the only airport in the Washington area with runways long enough to handle the supersonic transport Concorde, seen in the foreground.

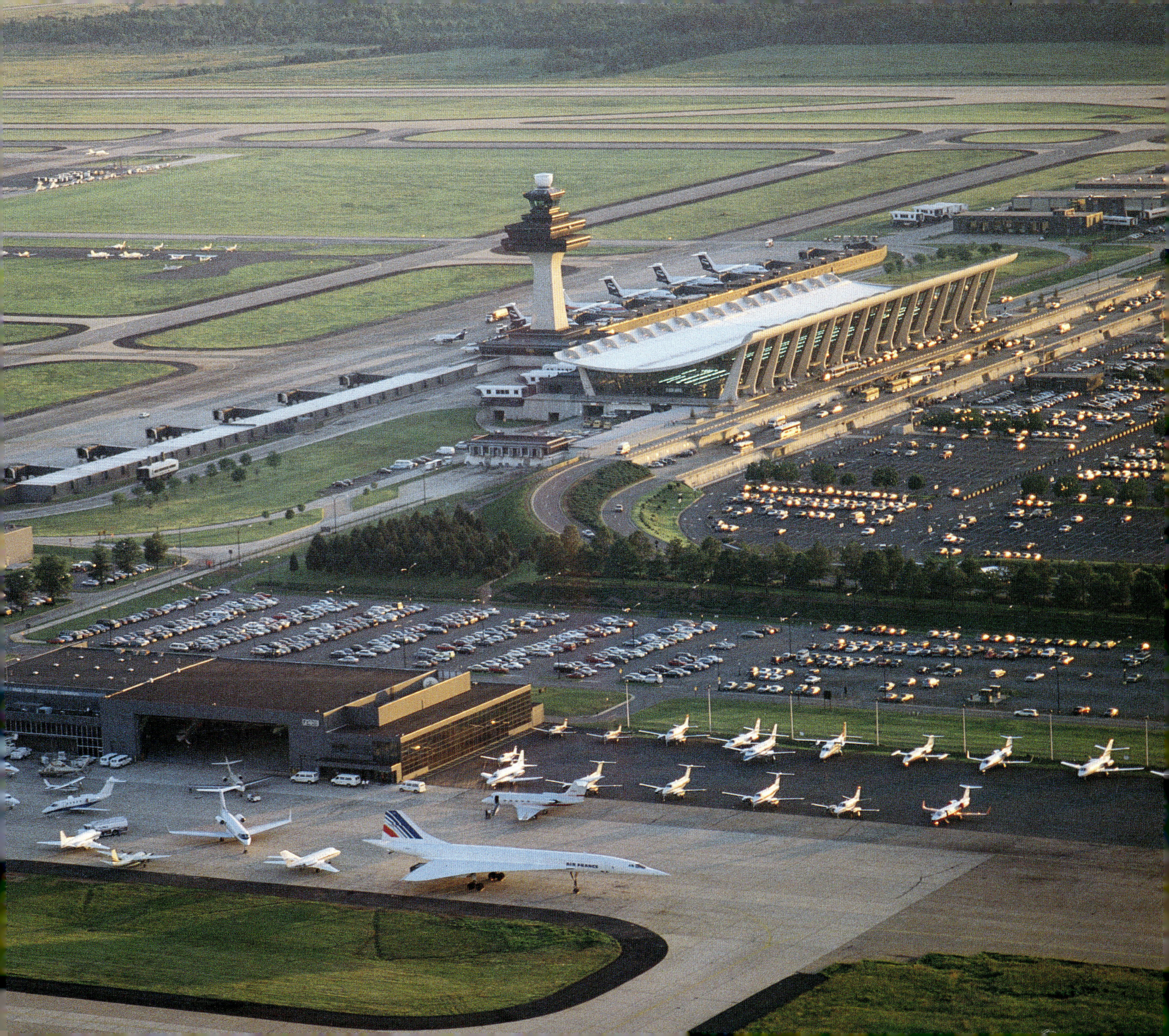
AIR FRANCE

▲▶ F-4 fighter jets and Air Force One at Andrews Air Force Base, Maryland. Part of 129 military aircraft housed at Andrews, the F-4s are used by pilots of the D.C. National Guard during monthly training exercises. Their exhaust created the black scorch marks seen on the concrete pad.

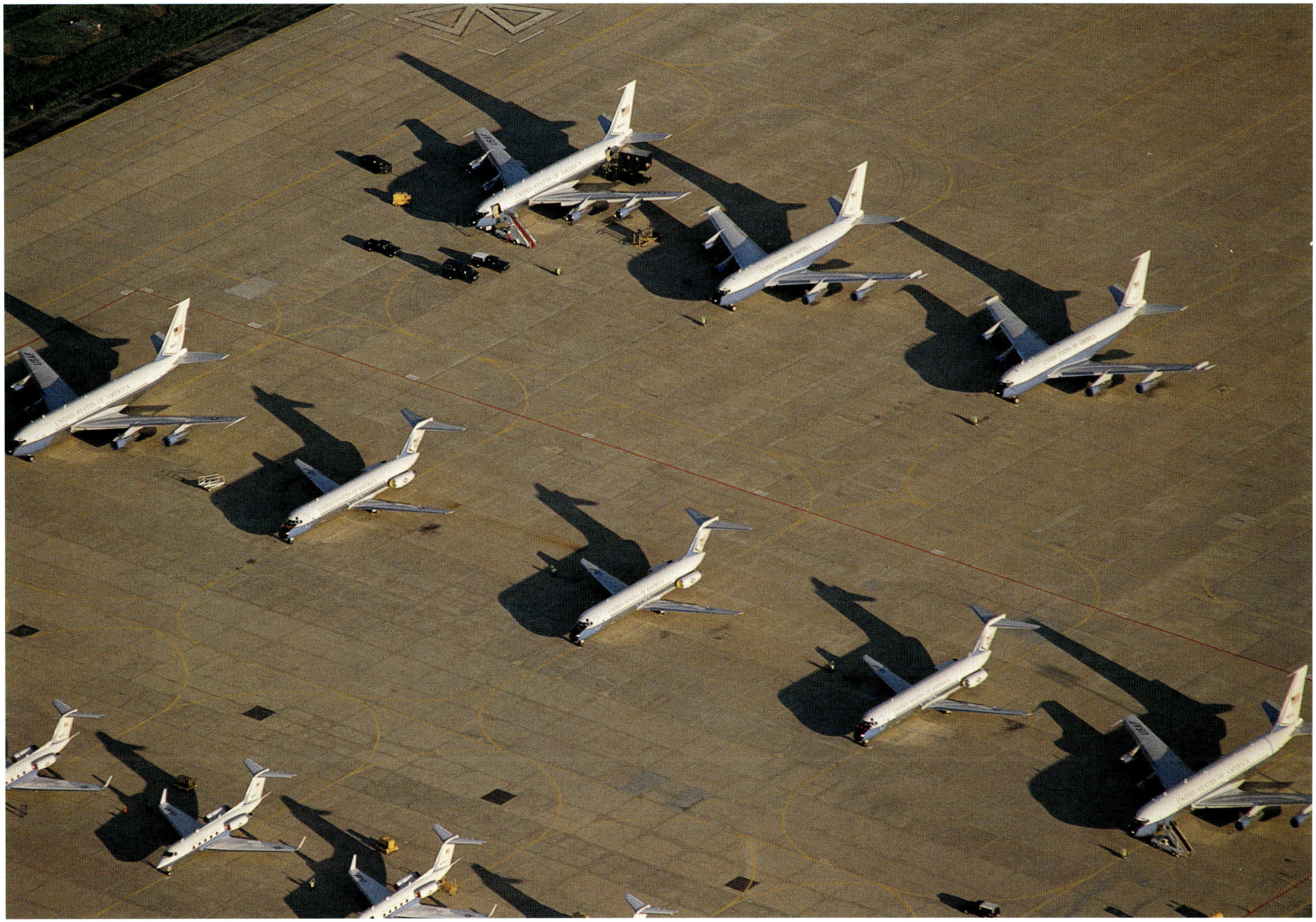

▶Andrews Air Force Base, Maryland. A Cessna 152 puts down at Andrews. More than 400 planes take off or land here every day.

100

▲ Middleburg Training Center, Virginia. Built by Paul Mellon on 126 acres, the equestrian center is a commercial training facility for what could become a common sight in the Old Dominion; Virginians voted in November 1988 to allow counties to institute pari-mutuel betting on horse races.

▲ Fort Washington, Maryland. The first defensive structure on this site, which was selected by George Washington in 1795, was Fort Warburton, built in 1808. Abandoned in the War of 1812 without a shot being fired from it, the original stronghold was replaced in 1822 with Fort Washington, following a design by Pierre Charles L'Enfant. The fortification is maintained today by the National Park Service.

▶ Mount Vernon, Virginia. Situated directly across the Potomac River from Fort Washington, Mount Vernon is the ancestral home of George Washington. The core of the main house was begun by George's father Augustine and completed in 1735; George added the dormers and cupola to the mansion during 1773. Mount Vernon is named after British Admiral Edward Vernon, under whom Lawrence Washington, George's brother, once served.

103

▲▶ Dulles Access Road and Maryland suburb. With construction of major highways such as the "Beltway" and the Dulles Access Road has come a new phenomenon: the totally suburban worker and dweller. As recently as 1980, about 40 percent of area jobs were in downtown Washington. By the year 2010 that figure is expected to drop below 30 percent.

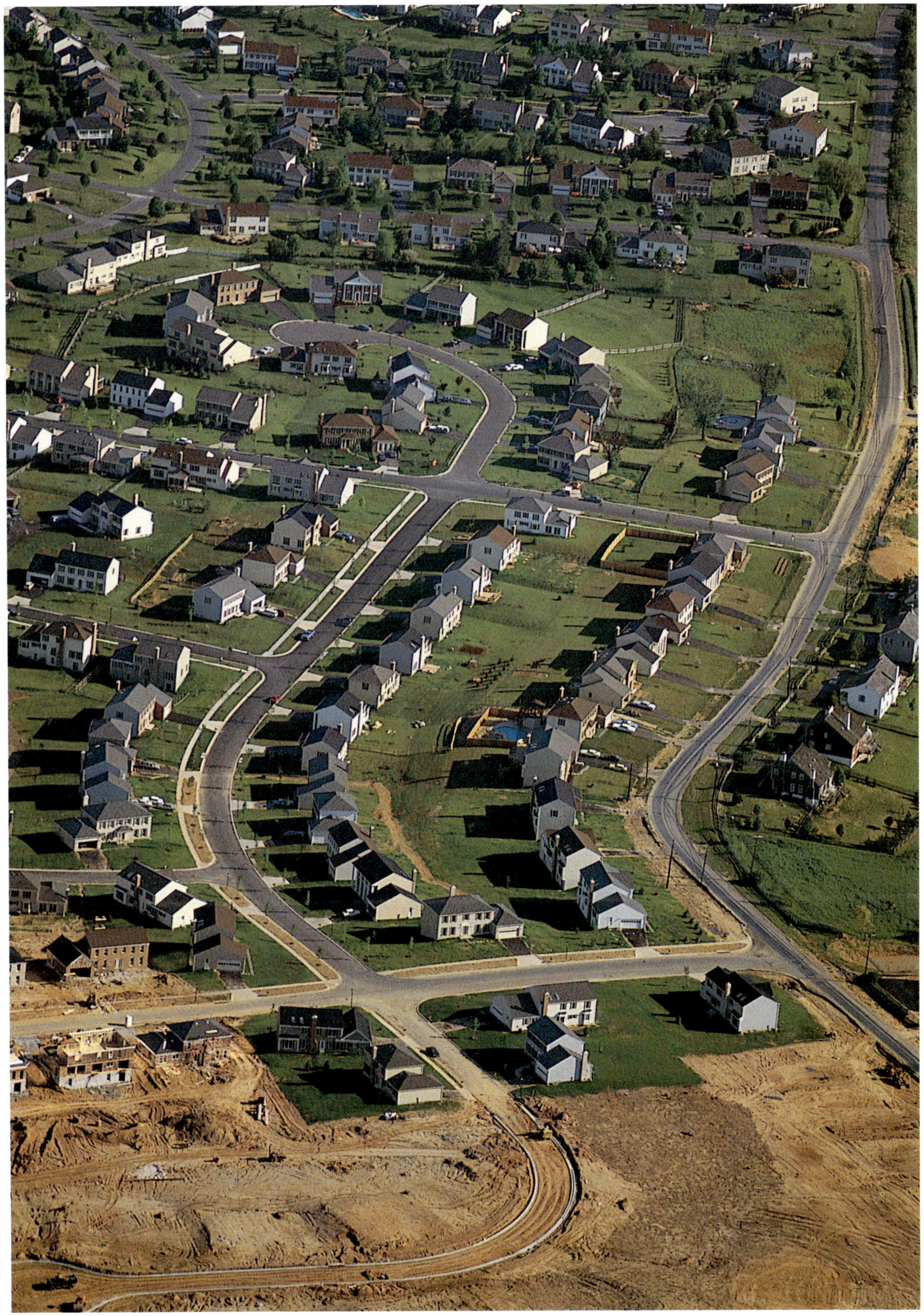

▲ Great Falls, Virginia. Located west of Washington on the Potomac River, the Great Falls region accounts for a third of the 150-foot drop in elevation that the river makes as it flows toward the Chesapeake Bay and sea level. In one second, nearly 12,000 cubic feet of water — drained from more than 11,000 square miles — tumble over the boulders here.

▲Sully Plantation at Chantilly, Virginia. Richard Bland Lee, Virginia's first congressman and the uncle of Robert E. Lee, raised his family here before selling the plantation to a cousin and moving to Alexandria, Virginia. Now a park, the plantation is one of five area houses once belonging to the Lee family that are open to the public.

▲▶ Northern Virginia's Catesby Farm and suburbs. A private horse training center, Catesby Farm is owned by Bahman Batmanghelidj, president of the Batman Corporation development firm. About 20 horses are kept in the stable. The small ring in front of it is used for breaking horses. In 1985 there were about 300,000 households located more than three miles outside the Beltway and within 20 miles of the center of the region. By the year 2010 that figure should double.

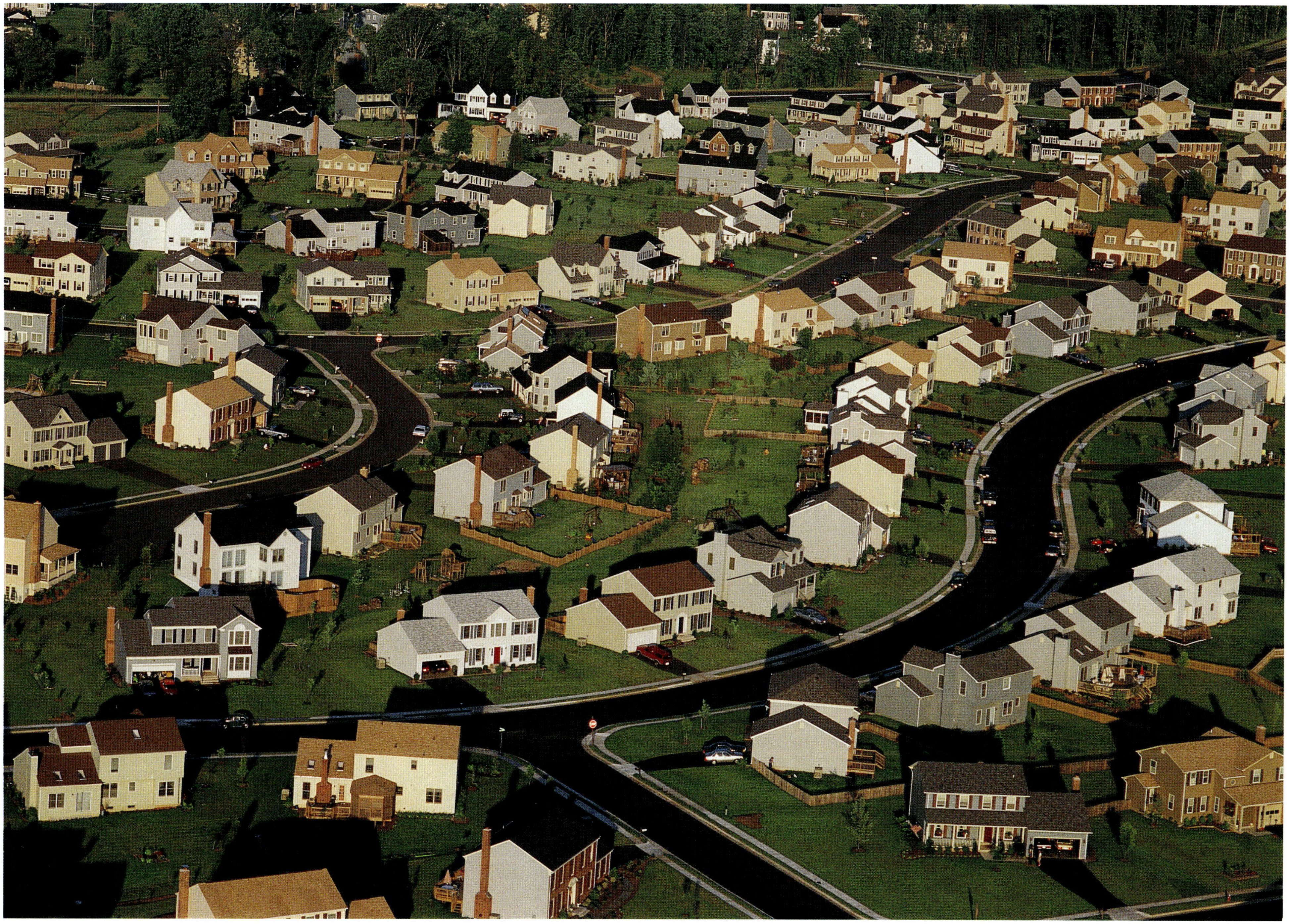

▲ Lorton Reformatory, Virginia. In jurisdictional terms, Lorton Reformatory is about as odd as a penal institution can be: a District of Columbia prison that sits on Virginia land acquired by the federal government in 1910.

▲Rifle range at Ft. Meade, Virginia. A red flag flying near the observation tower would mean that the range is operational. Here it is silent.

▲U.S. Naval Academy's Bancroft Hall in Annapolis, Maryland. One of the largest dormitories in the nation, Bancroft Hall has been called home by every midshipman to attend the academy since it opened in 1845. Appropriately, its dimensions are Pentagonesque, with 1,873 resident rooms, five miles of corridors, and 38 acres of floor space. Its name immortalizes George Bancroft, Secretary of the Navy for one year during the administration of James Polk.

▶"Main Street" in Annapolis, Maryland. Clogged with yachts and other pleasure craft in the summer, the watery avenue reverts back to its working origins in cold weather when the fishing boats and oystermen sail in.

113

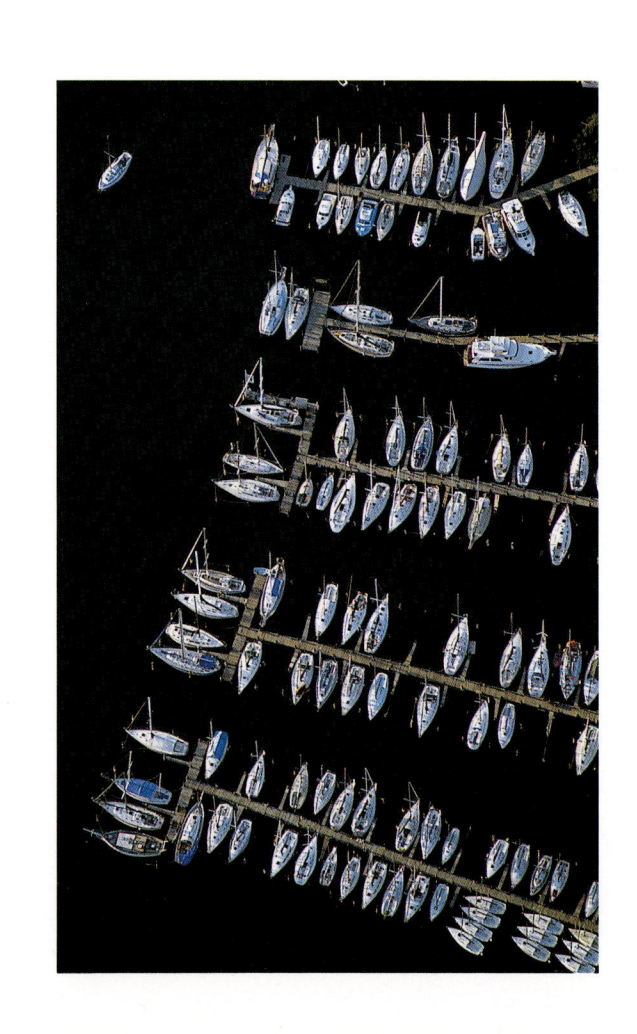

▶▶Annapolis, Maryland. Founded in 1649 by Puritans exiled from Virginia, the Maryland capital was first known as the city of Providence. Renamed in 1694 to honor British Princess (later Queen) Anne, Annapolis within the year became the seat of the British royal government in America.

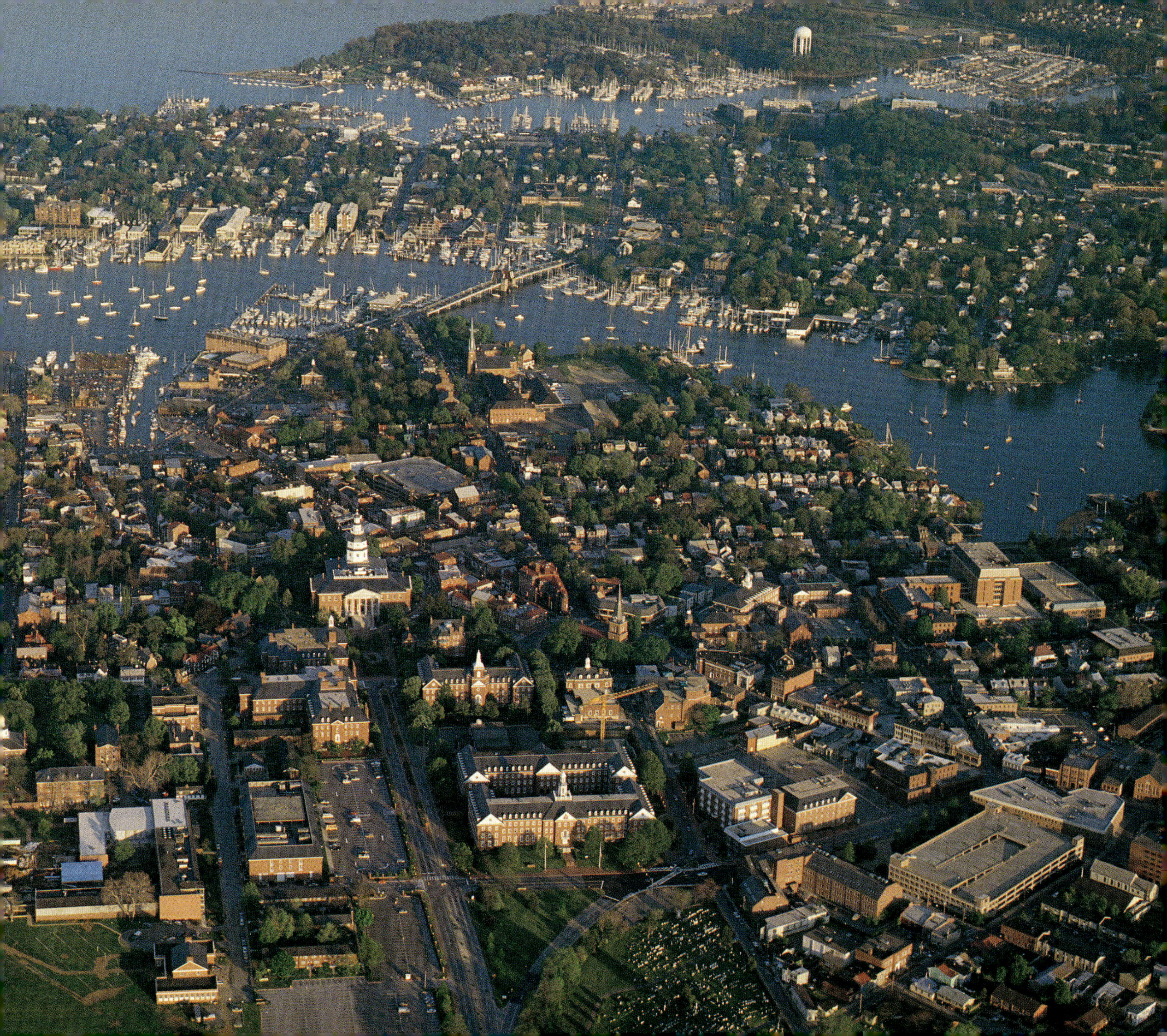

▲Jessup Automobile Distribution Center in Anne Arundel County, Maryland. Located on the main line of the Chessie System and owned by the railroad's parent CSX Corporation, the center receives new cars from manufacturing plants all over the nation. Vehicles are then doled out to dealerships in the Baltimore-Washington area or sent to the Port of Baltimore for export. Its standard inventory of 4,000 cars—parked on 45 acres—turns over about every three days.

▲Chesapeake Bay, Maryland. The bay, which cuts off the Eastern Shore of Maryland and Virginia from the mainland, is a popular location for oyster and crab fishing.

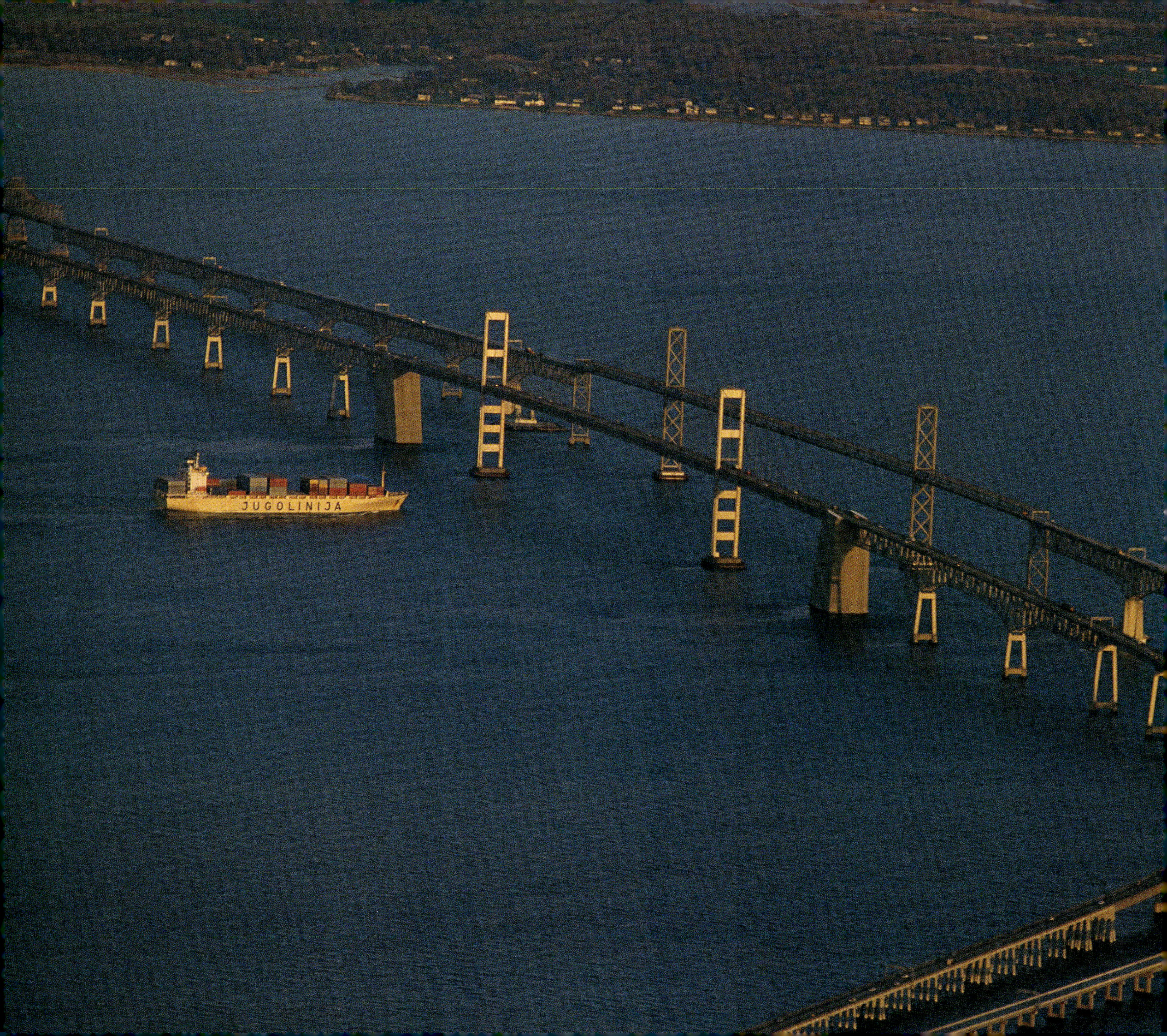
JUGOLINIJA

◀ Chesapeake Bay Bridge, Maryland. Opened in 1952, the steel arch bears the official name of William Preston Lane Memorial Bridge. Lane was Maryland's governor from 1947 to 1951. Four miles long from Sandy Point on the mainland of Maryland to Kent Island off the Eastern Shore, the bridge rises to 186.5 feet above the water. Here, a Yugoslavian freighter heads from the Port of Baltimore out to sea under the bridge.

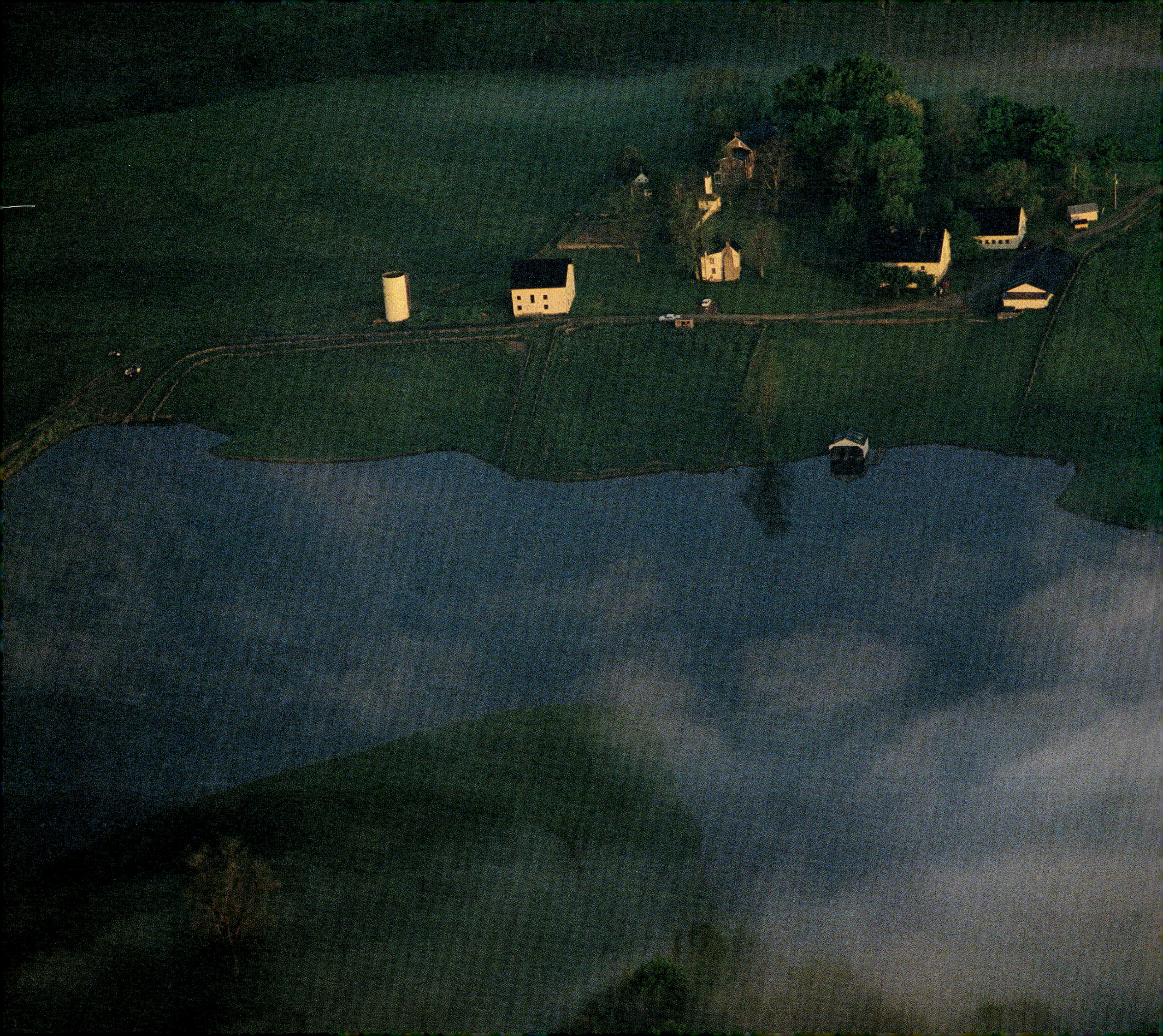

◀ Middleburg, Virginia. In his poem "To the Virginian Voyage," Michael Drayton wrote that Virginia was "Earth's only paradise...." Ironically, he died in London in 1631, having seen Earth's only paradise with nothing more than his inner eye.

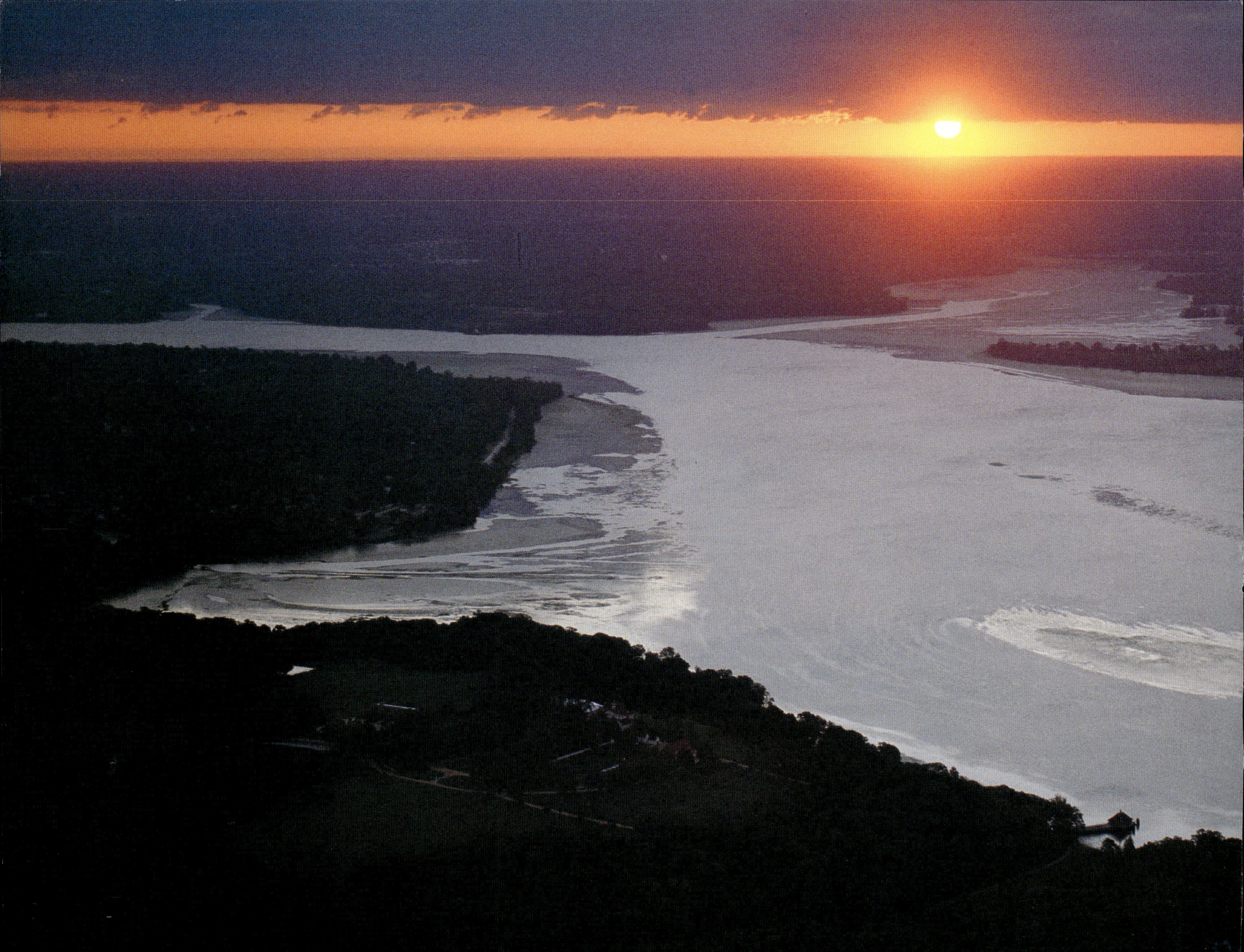

◀ Potomac River, looking east from high above Mount Vernon, Virginia.

The publisher wishes to extend a special thanks to
J.D. Quale and the staff at THE WASHINGTONIAN Magazine.